A Literary Friendship

Edited and with an Introduction by

Bruce Whiteman

A Literary Friendship

The Correspondence of

Ralph Gustafson and W. W. E. Ross

ECW PRESS

CANADIAN CATALOGUING IN PUBLICATION DATA

Gustafson, Ralph, 1909-
    A literary friendship

Bibliography: p.
ISBN 0-920802-57-5

1. Gustafson, Ralph, 1909-   2. Ross, W.W.E. (William Wrightson
Eustace), 1894-1966.   3. Poets, Canadian (English) —
Correspondence.*   I. Ross, W.W.E. (William Wrightson Eustace), 1894-
1966. II. Whiteman, Bruce, 1952-   III. Title.

PS8513.U8Z545 1984   C811′.54   C84-099171-0
PR9199.3.G8Z495 1984

This book has been published with the help of a grant from the Arts
Research Board, McMaster University. Additional grants were made available
from the Ontario Arts Council and The Canada Council.

A Literary Friendship was designed by The Dragon's Eye Press, typeset by
Imprint, and printed by The Porcupine's Quill.

"On Reading Certain Poems and Epistles of Irving Layton and Louis Dudek,"
by A.J.M. Smith, is reprinted by permission of McClelland and Stewart, The
Canadian Publishers.

Published by ECW PRESS, 307 Coxwell Avenue,
Toronto Ontario.

For Ralph and Betty, with affection

Register of Locations

University of Saskatchewan Library:
   #1-31, 33, 35-48, 50-51, 55, 58.

University of Toronto Library:
   32, 34, 49, 52-54, 56-57, 59, 61, 63-64.

Queen's University Archives:
   60, 62.

Introduction

When Ralph Gustafson first wrote to W.W.E. Ross in 1940 (in a letter now lost) to inquire, apparently, about his published work to date, Canadian poetry was poised on the brink of a Renaissance. Gustafson's own *Anthology of Canadian Poetry*, which he compiled for the then very young Penguin Books, was perhaps the first solid evidence of that renewal of activity. (It was published in England on 23 April 1942 and on 6 June in North America.) Within a period of twelve months, three significant magazines were established: *Contemporary Verse* (edited by Alan Crawley, September 1941), *Preview* (edited by Patrick Anderson, March 1942), and *First Statement* (edited by John Sutherland, August 1942). If one extends the focus to include the entire period of the war years, one finds the first book publications of A.J.M. Smith, A.M. Klein, Earle Birney, Patrick Anderson, and Irving Layton among others. As *New Provinces* had introduced the new poets of the 30s in the previous decade, so *Unit of Five*, in 1944, brought the work of several young poets before the already much diminished public for contemporary writing. Both books were financial failures for their publishers, but they were important aesthetically and prophetic of future reputations. All in all, it is remarkable in retrospect how fruitful and important the war years were.

Though it has been to some extent ignored by literary historians, the Gustafson anthology was a signal one. Previous anthologies had been filled, by and large, with what A.J.M.Smith once called maple fudge[1] — poetry that was vacuously nationalistic, proudly anachronistic, unashamedly sentimental, and various combinations of all three of these qualities. Gustafson himself described the field in 1945:

> There are a few good anthologies representing the best poetry that Canada has produced; there are also several bad anthologies which, while inevitably including some durable examples of our best poets, have been made with little evidence of discrimination and proportion. These latter volumes have done a disservice to Canadian poetry. From them, one

1 A.J.M. Smith, "Canadian Anthologies, New and Old," *University of Toronto Quarterly*, 11, No. 4 (July 1942), 458.

2 Ralph Gustafson, *Poetry and Canada* (Ottawa: Canadian Legion Educational Services, 1945), p. 14.

3 S. Morgan-Powell complained that Lanigan's poem "is not poetry, and has no place in any anthology that claims to print only poetry that is alive." See "New Anthology Presents an Admirable Selection," *Montreal Star*, 25 July 1942, p. 18. W. A. Deacon predicted that readers over 45 "will be amazed, and may inquire sadly why such long-standing favourites as Pauline Johnson were not held worthy of inclusion." See "Penguin Canadian Anthology Stresses Work of New Poets," *The Globe and Mail*, 6 June 1942, p. 9. Pauline Johnson was omitted because her publishers demanded too high a fee for her work.

4 Alan Crawley, "Notes on Some Reading," *Contemporary Verse*, 2, No. 5 (Sept. 1942), 16.

5 Ralph Gustafson, "The Story of the Penguin," *Canadian Poetry: Essays, Documents, Reviews*, No. 12 (Spring-Summer 1983), pp. 74-75. J. E. Morpurgo, in *Allen Lane, King Penguin: A Biography* (London: Hutchinson, 1979), several times remarks on Lane's preference for gentlemen's agreement over signed contract. Gustafson was to come to grief over this habit when he compiled a follow-up volume to *Canadian Accent*. The manuscript was

would conclude that Canada has produced little besides derivative verses in the fashion of Keats and Tennyson.[2]

It was Gustafson's double achievement to prepare the first anthology that both represented the classics in a stringent and uncompromising fashion, and concentrated on the moderns, some of whose work had not yet appeared in book form. Naturally not every reviewer felt that his weightings were astute in all respects; but even those critics who bewailed the exclusion of Pauline Johnson or the inclusion of "The Ahkoond of Swat" came out, on balance, in praise of the book.[3] The moderns themselves, and their supporters, knew that the anthology was "an important event in Canadian literature."[4]

The *Anthology of Canadian Poetry* was very much a war book, in circumstance if not in spirit. The Canadian government was interested in commissioning large editions of inexpensive books for the entertainment and edification of the troops, and a contract was made with Penguin Books to this end. Colonel Wilfrid Bovey, director of the extra-mural relations programme of McGill University, was chairman during the war years of the Canadian Legion Educational Services, the group through which books were made available to members of the Armed Services. (In used bookstores, one can still find copies of Canadian books with the C.L.E.S. stamp on the title-page.) Bovey knew Allen Lane, the director of Penguin, and he had read Gustafson's two books of verse published in the 1930s. Bovey put the publisher in touch with Gustafson, who was working in 1940 in New York City for the British Information Services, and without a contract but with Lane's encouragement, Gustafson began to work on the anthology.[5]

In the New York Public Library, he found some poems of W. W. E. Ross in *The Dial* (1928) and in *Poetry* (1934). Though praised by Marianne Moore as "conspicuously one of the writers of this day,"[6] in 1940 Ross was to all intents and purposes unknown as a poet to the majority of his countrymen. He had published two books — *Laconics* in 1930 and *Sonnets* in 1932 — but both were printed privately and went largely unnoticed; and his periodical appearances were few and without exception in American rather than Canadian magazines. Ross was interested in imagism and surrealism at a time when neither had yet attracted much notice in Canada. (Raymond Souster would later call him "the first modern Canadian poet" in the dedication to *New Wave Canada*.) His spare, unromantic verses of the Canadian northland, many of them written in 1928 and collected in *Laconics*, were among the earliest evidences that writers like Moore, cummings, Pound and Williams were being read and digested north of the forty-ninth parallel. His work was contemporary with that of Raymond Knister and Dorothy Livesay; but he was a scientist rather than a professional writer, and was largely unconcerned about publication and reputation. His inclusion in Gustafson's Penguin anthology brought him before a large public for the first time; but even at that, a representative selection of his poetry did not appear until 1968, two years after his death.

The correspondence began circumspectly. Gustafson was going through the harrying process of deciding on the contents of the Penguin book and seeking permission for the use of the poems he wanted. Though he gave no intimation of it in these early letters to Ross, he was meeting a good deal of resistance on some sides. His negotiations with publishers were in many cases protracted and antagonistic. No better sense of the situation can be given than by quoting from a letter written to Gustafson by Lorne Pierce during the course of a long correspondence over an extensive list of poems whose copyright belonged to the Ryerson Press:

> There is a definite feeling in Toronto, among the publishers, that this anthology should be prohibited because of the fact that it would undersell every other anthology in the market, copyright for which has cost enormous sums [...]

> Every book in which these poems have appeared — the poems which you have selected — has represented a financial loss. Now Penguin, on the pretense of getting these out for the troops, winnows these rich holdings and presents them in an anthology with which no Canadian publisher can hope to compete. The series has had a vicious effect, in some respects, on legitimate publishing, so I can understand the attitude of the other publishers in town.[7]

Ross, of course, put up no such barriers as the commercial publishers did. He not only gave his blessing; he also mentioned Raymond Knister's name to Gustafson and passed on some biographical and bibliographical information about him.

After these first few letters the correspondence lapsed for some sixteen months. In May of 1943, Gustafson wrote to send Ross a copy of the Canadian issue of *Voices*, Harold Vinal's New York-based little magazine, and to inquire about permission to use a Ross poem in another editorial project, the *Little Anthology of Canadian Poets* (as it would be called) which New Directions was to publish. A longer exchange of letters now began. Books and manuscripts were sent for inspection, and the two poets traded critical comments on each other's work and on the work of some of their

completed early in 1948, but it was never published. Colonel Bovey is mentioned in John Glassco's *Memoirs of Montparnasse*, where he is referred to as Colonel Birdlime (Toronto: Oxford Univ. Press, 1970, p. 3).

6 Marianne Moore, "Modern Thoughts in Disguise," *Poetry* [Chicago], 42, No. 2 (May 1933), 114.

7 Lorne Pierce to Ralph Gustafson, letter of 27 Jan. 1941 (Gustafson Papers, University of Saskatchewan Library).

contemporaries. In his letter of 6 June 1943, Gustafson first mentioned *Canadian Accent*, the anthology, mostly of prose, which he had undertaken for Penguin in 1942. From among a large amount of material which Ross sent to him, a group of thirteen prose poems was chosen for inclusion under the title "Distillates." The choice surprised Ross; he thought them "the very last things I should until recently have ever expected to be chosen for a volume of popular circulation." But "Distillates" not only represented an aspect of Ross's work of which the poetry anthology gave no hint; it also provided a change of weight and pace in *Canadian Accent* in the way that the few poems included similarly did. Unlike the *Anthology of Canadian Poetry, Canadian Accent* was never published in Canada. It was Gustafson's feeling that William Collins Sons, who were Penguin's Canadian distributors and printers, stalled on *Canadian Accent* (as they also refused to reprint the poetry anthology after the third impression of August 1944) in order that their own anthology, *A Pocketful of Canada*, could have a clearer field. (Indeed, Gustafson protested to Collins about the similarity of the contents of the anthology to his own.) Ross's letters certainly show that the Penguin book was not easily to be found in Toronto bookstores.

With Ross's compliments on the anthology the first major series of letters ended. A few letters were exchanged in 1947 and 1952, these occasioned by requests which Gustafson received from publishers to reprint some of Ross's work. The correspondence picked up again in 1956, some months after the two poets had met for the first time at the Kingston writers' conference masterminded by F. R. Scott. By this time Gustafson had begun to work on a complete revision of the Penguin anthology, and his curiosity about Ross's work provoked the interesting letter of 23 September 1956, in which Ross described the genesis of his northern poems. The series of letters which constellates around the *Penguin Book of Canadian Verse* gives extensive evidence of Ross's knowledge of Canadian poetry and his care for detail, this latter the mark of the scientist perhaps. In light of the obvious technical expertise that he shows in his remarks about Gustafson's own poems, and the virtuoso interpretation which he gives of some lines of A.J.M. Smith, one is almost amused to find his over-modest avowal: "I find it hard to write *about* writing, not being in a university" (letter #38). Though Ross published very little critical writing, his series of parodies in the style of various poets ("Air With Variations") demonstrates his acute sense of style as well as his powers as a poetic mimic. If some of the occasional pieces which he sent to Gustafson with a letter from time to time are less interesting, all in all the letters corroborate Barry Callaghan's feeling that Ross's "insight into poetic discipline was acute .... There was just no question: Eustace knew what he was talking about. He had a first-rate critical mind."[8]

During the period when he was working on the Penguin book, Gustafson continued to live in New York, where he supported himself by freelancing. The publication of the anthology (20 November 1958 was the official date) signalled the beginning of a second stage in his career as a poet. He had published no books since *Flight Into Darkness* (1944), but the Penguin volume was followed two years later by *Rivers Among Rocks*, and after that (and following his return to Canada in 1963) other books of poetry appeared regularly. Ross sent a long letter of comment about the new anthology, of which he approved but which struck him less forcefully than the original *Anthology of Canadian Poetry*. This letter more or less closed the correspondence, though several briefer and not uninteresting ones followed it in the period up to 1964. Souster and Colombo speak of 1958 as the year in which Ross's last serious work was done,[9] and it is apparent from these final letters that his interest in poetry was declining, in part undoubtedly (though he does not mention this) because of illness.

Ralph Gustafson corresponded with a large number of Canadian writers during his New York years, in some cases desultorily and in some on a regular and long-term basis. The letters to and from Earle Birney, A.J.M. Smith and John Sutherland, for example, bulk larger than his correspondence with Eustace Ross, even allowing for the fact that there are a few letters to Ross of which Gustafson kept no copies. The correspondence with Ross is of particular interest, however, for a number of reasons. Ross's work is generally acknowledged by poets and critics as having an important place in the early development of modernism in Canada, and yet little study of the poetry has been made and even less is known about Ross's life.[10] Thus, when he says that he made an extensive study of Greek metres in the 1920s, or speaks of his intense interest in surrealism in the early 1930s, or remarks that he feels "much closer, mentally, to the medicine man than to Diderot" (letter #28), something important is added to our knowledge of the man and his work. It is apparent from these letters that Ross's life as a poet was to some extent an intermittent one, but that Gustafson's persistent interest in his work did a good deal to rouse him to further composition or to rework existing pieces. For Gustafson's part, the letters permit us access to the background of the important Penguin anthologies; a rationale of inclusion emerges, as well as some sense of the various problems which Gustafson encountered. Overall, and not the least interesting aspect of the correspondence, are the glimpses we are afforded of the literary history of the 40s and 50s, from the inside out as it were. It is a period which deserves more detailed investigation, and it is hoped that

8 W.W.E. Ross, *Shapes & Sounds: Poems of W.W.E. Ross*, ed. Raymond Souster and John Robert Colombo, with a Memoir by Barry Callaghan (Don Mills: Longmans Canada Ltd., 1968), p. 3.

9 Ross, p. 8

10 The only major study of Ross's poetry is that of Peter Stevens, "On W.W.E. Ross," *Canadian Literature*, No. 39 (Winter 1969), pp. 43-61. Of interest also is Michael Darling's editing of Ross's letters to A.J.M. Smith, "On Poetry and Poets: The Letters of W.W.E. Ross to A.J.M. Smith," *Essays on Canadian Writing*, No. 16 (Fall-Winter 1979-80), pp. 78-125.

the publication of these letters is a small step in that direction.

* * * *

In preparing these letters for publication it is a reading text that I have kept in mind. To this end I have tried to keep the annotations brief and to a minimum, and as much as possible the editor's hand has been kept from sight. Obvious slips of the pen (or typewriter) have been emended silently, and only occasionally have I inserted a word (in square brackets) when its unintentional absence obscured the sense. The transcription of the correspondence is based largely on files in the Ralph Gustafson papers in the University of Saskatchewan Library. These letters have been checked against those which are also present in the W. W. E. Ross papers in the University of Toronto Library, and the Saskatchewan collection has been supplemented by the addition of sixteen letters found only in the Ross archive. Two further letters have been added from the collection of Gustafson material at Queen's University Archives. A few of Gustafson's letters exist only in the form of carbon copies, and in those cases I have supplied a closing where, in the original, it would have been written in ink. (All but two of Gustafson's letters are typed, while Ross's are sometimes typed and sometimes in holograph.) The bibliography at the end lists all of those works referred to either in the letters themselves or in the introduction and notes.

I am grateful to Ralph Gustafson both for his invitation to edit this correspondence and for his assistance and encouragement. Mary Lowry Ross kindly consented to the publication of W. W. E. Ross's side of the correspondence. Glen Makahonuk of the University of Saskatchewan Library provided copies of the letters and assisted my editorial work by answering various questions which arose, and the Thomas Fisher Rare Book Library of the University of Toronto kindly furnished me with copies of the letters in the Ross papers. Copies of the two letters in the Queen's University Archives were made for me by Mrs. Shirley Spragge.

For help with some of the annotations I would like to thank the following: Mr. Robert Bertholf, Mr. Jack David, J. M. Dent & Sons (Canada) Ltd., Mrs. Audrey Sutherland, and Yale University Library. "On Reading Certain Poems and Epistles of Irving Layton and Louis Dudek," from *The Classic Shade: Selected Poems* by A. J. M. Smith is used by permission of The Canadian Publishers, McClelland and Stewart Limited, Toronto. Horace Gregory's poem "Hellbabies" is quoted with the permission of the estate of Horace Gregory. The excerpt from Lorne Pierce's letter to Ralph Gustafson is used with permission of the estate of Lorne Pierce and the University of Saskatchewan Library.

Assistance toward the publication of this book was provided by the Arts Research Board of McMaster University, to whom the editor proffers his thanks.

Bruce Whiteman
April 1984

I

62 Delaware Ave.,
Toronto, Ontario, Canada,
Nov. 14/40

Ralph Gustafson, Esq.,
70 Central Park W.,
N.Y.C.

Dear Mr. Gustafson,—

The two books *Sonnets* and *Laconics* were not put out for sale, and only a few review copies etc were distributed. So I am sending you copies. Please dispose of them otherwise than by sending them back, as it only means an annoying trip to the Customs House.

What has been printed to date, then, is

Dial, April 1928 — Small group.

Dial, August 1928 — Large Group (corrected version of one is on p. 30 of *Sonnets*.)

Laconics — 1930

Sonnets — 1932

Poetry, July 1934 — Large group.

New Directions 1937 — Large group of prose pieces along surrealist lines, but written in 1932.

(*Fifth Floor Window*, May 1932 — 2 similar pieces, one also in *New Directions*).[1]

Apart from the 2 cases cited, there is no duplication in the above items. I believe the *Dial, Poetry*, (and *New Directions*) are on file in the N.Y. Public Library.

Yours sincerely,
W. W. E. Ross

I hope you are including Raymond Knister,[2] (drowned in 1932). See *Canadian Forum*, September 1932.[3]

1 W. W. E. Ross, "Two Poems," *The Dial*, 84 (April 1928), 289-90; "Seven Poems," *The Dial*, 85 (Aug. 1928), 107-10; *Laconics* (Ottawa: Overbrook Press, 1930); *Sonnets* (Toronto: The Heaton Publishing Co., 1932); "Irrealistic Verses," *Poetry* [Chicago], 44, No. 4 (July 1934), 179-84; "Distillates," *New Directions in Poetry & Prose 1937*, ed. James Laughlin IV (Norfolk: New Directions, 1937), pp. 125-29; "Example" and "Hypno II," *Fifth Floor Window*, I, No. 4 (May 1932), n. pag.

2 Raymond Knister died on 29 Aug. 1932.

3 Leo Kennedy, "Raymond Knister," *The Canadian Forum*, Sept. 1932, pp. 459-61.

2

62 Delaware Ave.,
Toronto, Ontario, Canada,
Nov. 27th, 1940.

Dear Mr. Gustafson,—

While I never knew Raymond Knister [inserted: pronounced Knīster] (as I find it is spelled) I learned something about him from a friend. He never published a book of his verse, but probably would have done so. He was about to return to Toronto to live when he was drowned in the fall of 1932.

Immediately before his death a group of his poems appeared in *The Canadian Forum*[1] along with an article by Leo Kennedy. I have copied out the group in its entirety. From the article I condense as follows:—

A group of seven poems appeared in the *Midland* of December 1921.[2] Enough poems have appeared in American poetry magazines to form a small volume but they are still uncollected. He lived twenty years on an Ontario farm, died at 32. He worked on the *Midland*, also for *Poetry*. He placed short stories and poetry with *This Quarter*[3] (Paris, in the late twenties).

He had not become well-known and I am anxious to help make sure that he doesn't get overlooked, which might possibly happen as anthologists hereabouts show a tendency to follow a well-worn track.

Yours sincerely,
W. W. E. Ross

1 A group of nine poems by Knister appeared in *The Canadian Forum*, Sept. 1932, pp. 461-62.

2 A group of seven poems by Knister was published in the *Midland*, No. 8 (Dec. 1922), pp. 329-32.

3 Knister published a poem, "A Row of Horse Stalls," in *This Quarter*, 1, No. 2 (1925), 30, and two stories, "Elaine," in 1, No. 1 (1925), 160-66, and "The Fate of Mrs. Lucier," in 2, No. 2 (1925), 172-81.

3

Apartment 7A
70 Central Park West
New York, N.Y.
January 13, 1941

Dear Mr Ross,

My Penguin *Anthology of Canadian Poetry* is now complete.

I have decided to include, if you will allow me, five poems of yours:
"The Walk," "Fish," "The Saws Were Shrieking" (all from *Laconics*),
"Blindness" (from *Sonnets*), and "The Driver" (from *Poetry* for July 1934).

If this is agreeable would you write me granting me copyright permission for Canada, England, and the United States to reprint these poems in
the Penguin Books Ltd.'s anthology?

This concerns, of course, only the right for these poems' appearance in
the Penguin Anthology — other dispensation remains with you.

As I have to send off my MS to England immediately, may I hear from
you by return?

Perhaps you could help me in my search to find out who holds the
copyright on Raymond Knister's poems — or isn't there any? I don't wish
to trespass. Perhaps you would know Mrs. Knister's address (she has
removed from Toronto)? And was he born at Blenheim, Ont. in 1900?[1] I
hate to trouble you further, but of course want everything clear.

Would you send me data for my Biographical Notes on yourself? *Viz:*
year and place of birth; where educated, etc.

With all best wishes and many thanks for your kind cooperation.

Sincerely,
Ralph Gustafson

[1] Knister was born on 27 May
1899 at Ruthven, near Wind-
sor, Ontario.

4

62 Delaware Ave.,
Toronto, Jan. 15/41

Dear Mr. Gustafson,—

Of course you may print the five pieces you mention, in the Penguin
Anthology.

Mrs. Knister was in Toronto (visit) three years ago, I know, and was then
living in Port Dover, Ontario, where her people live (or that neighbourhood)
and where she had lived since 1932. So I think it very likely she is still there.
She has made a collection of her husband's poems, I have been told.

Raymond Knister was 32 years old in 1932; so almost certainly born in
1900, and as the name "Blenheim" is familiar to me and others in that con-

nection it is almost certainly his birthplace. As regards copyright, it is very unlikely that there is any (they appeared scattered in magazines only), though it might be best to get Mrs. Knister's permission, which I think would certainly be granted, as my recollection from talks about them both is that she is quite anxious to keep his work from oblivion.

Yours sincerely,
W. W. E. Ross

P.S. I was born at Peterborough, Ontario in 1894; graduate in chemistry of University of Toronto.[1] Since 1923 on scientific staff of Canadian Government.

1 Ross was born on 14 June 1894 in Peterborough. He graduated from the University of Toronto in 1914.

5

Apartment 7A
70 Central Park West
New York, N.Y.
January 17, 1941

Dear Mr Ross,

Many thanks for your letter of the fifteenth and for your authorization to include your poems in the Penguin Anthology.

Leo Kennedy thought Mrs Knister was living in Port Dover (or Port Hope) — and so I have written to the Postmaster at both places in my effort to clear the copyright of his poems from Mrs Knister. I am hoping to hear in time. I'm very grateful for all the trouble you have taken over this matter.

Many thanks too for including the data for my Bibliographical Notes.

With best wishes,

Sincerely,
[Ralph Gustafson]

6

Dear Mr Ross,

New Directions Press has told me that they are going ahead with the Canadian Issue which I edited for one in their series on monthly Poets of the Year. It will be called *Canadian Poets 1943*. I included your "Falling Water" — and trust this is all right?[1]

I thought you might like a copy of the Canadian issue of *Voices*.[2] With best wishes,

Ralph Gustafson

1 W. W. E. Ross, "Falling Water," in *A Little Anthology of Canadian Poets*, ed. Ralph Gustafson (Norfolk: New Directions, 1943), n. pag.

2 The Canadian issue of *Voices*, edited by Gustafson, was No. 113 (Spring 1943). It did not contain any Ross poems.

7

62 Delaware Ave,
Toronto, Ontario,
May 14/43.

Dear Mr. Gustafson,—

Thank you for the copy of the Canadian issue of *Voices*. I had seen most of these pieces before, but among the others, appreciate especially some by Finch and also the sonnet by Smith, read only in passing hitherto.

Patrick Anderson of course calls for comment because of the amount of space given him. I associate him with the "fantaisistes," André Salmon for example. (I was more impressed by Max Jacob than by Salmon, or Apollinaire either). One might be inclined to call him somewhat "surrealistic" because of a certain verbal elasticity, but I find in him no trace of the search through the subconscious that marks surrealism or did in its strongest phase.

I might make something of D. C. Scott's "A Dream" if it wasn't so prettified.[1]

I wonder if E. K. Brown meant what he said (*Toronto Quarterly*) when he stated he would have included one of Pratt's narratives in full in your Pelican Anthology.[2] If he had said Earle Birney's "David"[3] there might have been

1 Duncan Campbell Scott, "A Dream," *Voices*, No. 113 (Spring 1943), pp. 6-8.

2 E. K. Brown's review of Gustafson's *Anthology of Canadian Poetry (English)* was in the *University of Toronto Quarterly*, 12, No. 3 (April 1943), 311-12.

3 Earle Birney, "David," *The Canadian Forum*, Dec. 1941, pp. 274-76; collected in *David and Other Poems* (Toronto: Ryerson, 1942).

more point to the suggestion. For my part, I am afraid I can't properly "see" Pratt's writing, probably because I have never felt any influence from it. It seems to me mostly pretty expert word-juggling and rhyming.

You may of course use "Falling Water" in the New Directions booklet.

Yours sincerely,
W. W. E. Ross
————————————————————

8
————————————————————

May 21, 1943

Dear Mr Ross,

Many thanks for your permission to use "Falling Water" in the New Directions booklet.

I would have liked a new poem or two from you for the *Voices* effort — but haven't seen any appearances of yours. Are you writing anything these days? I think Anderson has a great deal behind his bewildering prolificacy — acute observation and manipulation of language to communicate it. But he's like a baby without a skeleton. But where are the craftsmen in Canada anyway? 'Twould have been impossible to include a full Pratt narrative in the Penguin — or "David" either, as much as I would have liked to — if the poem had been written at the time, that is.

Would you care to have a copy of *Lyrics Unromantic*?[1] Its technique, may interest.

Sincerely,
[Ralph Gustafson]
————————————————————

1 Ralph Gustafson, *Lyrics Unromantic* (New York: L. F. White, 1942).

9

62 Delaware Ave.,
Toronto, Ontario
May 29/43.

Dear Mr. Gustafson,—

Thank you again, this time for *Lyrics Unromantic*. Nos. 1, 11, and 12, or
their first lines, come most readily to mind when I think of the book. (This is
my test, by the way, of contemporary work — retention of first lines in
memory). I think you have succeeded in putting a good deal of intensity into
these pieces.

Speaking of your work in general, as far as I have seen it, the "Epithalamium"[1] impresses me most. If the tropes seem too crowded on first reading,
they should clear themselves up eventually, — though not all have done so for
me, so far. Now this poem is of about the length I think is needed most in
Canadian verse — i.e. 100 lines more (perhaps considerably) or less. Concentration on form tends to brevity. Smith and Finch are examples. I think
longer poems are needed. Look at the weight "Tintern Abbey" pulls in
Wordsworth's work — nothing startling about the style, but it is long enough
to give Wordsworth a chance to say a lot about what he really thinks and
feels. (To say nothing of the "Immortality" Ode). It seems to me that a whole
lot of poets are effectively kept in memory by a few medium length pieces;
where a much greater number of short ones — though good — would elude
individual recollection. "David" seems to me a substantial contribution in that
respect. Here I don't mean rattling narratives like Masefield or Vachel
Lindsay.

I haven't submitted anything to magazines since 1938 (except mistakenly,
to *Contemporary Verse*, B.C., on Miss Livesay's suggestion).[2] Anything
printed in magazines was asked for, except at the start with the *Dial*. I have
been trying out some more recent things (1939 to date) on Marianne Moore.
If she shows sufficient approval of the last batch, now with her, I may think
of trying some of them out elsewhere.

Yours sincerely,
W. W. E. Ross

---

1 Ralph Gustafson, *Epithalamium in Time of War* (New
York: L. F. White, 1941).

2 None of Ross's work was
published in *Contemporary
Verse*. See the section of a
letter from him to Floris
McLaren quoted in Joan
McCullagh, *Alan Crawley and
Contemporary Verse* (Van-
couver: Univ. of British
Columbia Press, 1976), p. 15.

IO

June 6, 1943

Dear Mr Ross,

Many thanks for your letter — and most welcome the news of your writing. I look forward to the appearances. I regret not approaching you for the Canadian issue of *Voices*. The collection is the poorer for not having included you. I still have under fire a second Anthology for the Penguin people. Mostly prose this time — and which I call *Canadian Accent*. Would you care to send along some of your new work? I hope to include about eight or nine poems, Pratt, Smith, Scott, Klein ... (I hope to be able to pay contributors a little).[1]

I'm glad one or two of the *Lyrics Unromantic* are proving memorable. I agree with your test of memorable *language*. It proves form, and music, and a word-sequence with at least something of inevitability. So much of the Canadian writing leaves with me a *general* impression, a diffused emotion unsquared by the medium, or a sentiment without finality, or a finality without projection. In other words, liquidity without craft!

I confess to a joyful encrustation in *Epithalamium in Time of War*. I believe that its music will obviate its being a "difficult" poem. Its sound is its meaning, as well. But its wordage is concrete and concentrated. Highly formalized. But I think right for an epithalamium — with no time for the traditional leisure of the pastoral. However, whether it thus communicates, I cant tell. But it was a joyful job.

Another test, for Canadians, as you say, is the poem of a hundred lines, or less. Loquaciousness, and pleasurable loquaciousness, we have much of — Anderson, for instance. But of ability to master adequate form, I find little. Hambleton[2] is so cerebral that he doesnt exist below the chin (often); Marriott's "The Wind Our Enemy",[3] while the best thing she's done, is occasionally housekeeping rather than craftsmanship. The spinal cord needs the vertebrae. "David" is a fine contribution.

With best wishes,

Sincerely,
Ralph Gustafson

1 Ralph Gustafson, ed., *Canadian Accent: A Collection of Stories and Poems by Contemporary Writers from Canada* (Harmondsworth: Penguin, 1944). A group of prose poems by Ross is included under the title "Distillates" (pp. 63-66).

2 Ronald Hambleton's work first appeared in book form in *Unit of Five*, a small anthology which he edited for Ryerson Press in 1944. Gustafson included poems by him in the *Anthology of Canadian Poetry* and the Canadian issue of *Voices*.

3 Anne Marriott, *The Wind Our Enemy* (Toronto: Ryerson, 1939).

II

---

62 Delaware Ave.,
Toronto, Ontario
June 14/43.

Dear Mr. Gustafson,—

Taking advantage of your interest I have skimmed rather largely the cream (or scum) from my mss. of the last few years, picking out what seemed most familiar. If you should want anything for *Canadian Accent* you may have it, of course.

This anthology seems rather a formidable task, the prose I mean, and I shall be quite curious to see what you have made of it. Of course you may have dug up some young writers yet unprinted. Looking around from this particular point they are not very visible.

Did the *Anthology of Canadian Poetry* bring any interesting comment in the U.S.A. or England? I looked for a review of it in *Poetry* which I see sometimes but didn't find any.[1] I am interested now in several Canadian poets in the same way in which I have always been interested in a number of contemporary British and American poets, that is, on a genuinely competitive basis, with no extra allowance, so far as I am aware, for nationality.

Yours sincerely,
W. W. E. Ross

---

[1] No review of the *Anthology* was published in *Poetry*. The book was, however, reviewed widely in both England and the United States.

12

---

as from
70 Central Park West
New York, N.Y.
July 4, 1943

Dear Mr Ross,

Many thanks for letting me read the selections from your mss. Again, in many of the poems I found that cool, refreshing immediate quality which is no less vivid for its simplicity. I liked particularly "Close the Windows" from *Largo*; "Sounds," "Crystalline," [and] "Cicadas" from *Allegro*; and "Cedar-Leaf." The last, too, is well-rooted in Canada — though most of yours have a northness which is akin to me.

I thought I might use "Cedar-Leaf" in *Canadian Accent* — if that is agreeable. I would prefer (I think) "Close the Windows" — but I am a little troubled about

> It may do us harm,
> some think and are alarmed.

Somehow, for my part, the triple "at" echoes disturb the marvellous atmosphere you create. What do you think? Am I wrong?

This anthology indeed proves a formidable task — that is why it has been far too long on the fire cooking. Seasoned and original prose writers with something urgent to say seem far apart in Canada. I have a piece on Pratt by E. K. Brown, Edel on Canadian writing, Gelber on Canada comes of age, stories by Sinclair Ross, MacLennan, Marcuse, McConnell, Birney, [and] Sybil Hutchison. I need only one or two more good stories.

I enclose your ms. with many thanks. Any possibility of a volume from you one of these days? Would be glad to hear from you on "Close the Windows".

Sincerely,
[Ralph Gustafson]

B

62 Delaware Ave.,
Toronto Ontario,
July 10/43.

Dear Mr. Gustafson,—

In "Close the Windows," "It may do us ill" seems to me a substitute for "It may do us harm," raising the pitch a little. In the copy you saw there was a gap between "at" and "hand," which is an error in typing. No extra space is intended after "at".

Your liking the 3 pieces from *Allegro* is of great interest to me, because this particular form, along with the *Laconics* form, was the main product of my effort in 1925-26 to develop forms which were more "North American" than the standard English forms, and at the same time more definitely patterned rhythmically than "free verse". I went into the Greek metres pretty thoroughly at that time, as I remember. The difficulty was, — and still is — to arrive at a fresh form suitable for pieces of some length. I may possibly send down all the *Allegro* pieces for your inspection, sometime.

What quality will ultimately be recognized as distinctively Canadian in English-language verse is, I suppose, impossible to realize yet, fully. My impression is that your *Anthology of Canadian Poetry*, or, perhaps, I should say the second half of that anthology, is an approximation. I realized more fully the other day how well you had succeeded in gleaning some cleanliness (aesthetically speaking) from the Canadian poetry mess when I looked into a few of the collected works, Roberts' for example, — a disheartening experience, I must say.

Yours sincerely,
W. W. E. Ross

14

August 13, 1943

Dear Mr Ross,

I am sorry to have left your last letter unanswered so long. It greatly interested me. I have made the change in "Close the Windows". Another idea has struck me. I had occasion the other day to pick up *New Directions* 1937 and found therein your "Distillates". Can I bother you again? Have you anything of that nature for *Canadian Accent*? I'd hate to forego representing your poetry — but, as you suspected, I am having more than a deal of trouble to find adequate prose — and this venture is, of course, primarily prose. I thought I'd throw this idea out to you anyhow.

Do, if you will, send along *Allegro*. I should love to read it in entirety. I was interested in your original search for a form. You succeeded. But I am not so sure that anyone but yourself could weld it to their poetry — your quality of simplicity and suggestion and crystallineness, I mean.

I took unto myself your words on the Penguin Anthology. I dont think anyone had adequately appreciated the Augean Stables I swept to get a book with at least some crispness and cleanness to it. If you have just been through some of our Collected Poets — you will appreciate what I went through! My New Directions booklet is announced for October.

All the best, and may I hear from you about any prose?

[Ralph Gustafson]

15

62 Delaware Ave,
Toronto, Ontario,
Aug. 27/43.

Dear Mr. Gustafson,—

Again you have sent me to rummaging among dustcovered mss. I found your stimulating letter on returning from a summer cottage a few days ago, and have been a little slow in replying because I came back with some sort of "bug" and a temperature.

I thought the best I could do would be to send you "Distillates" in its (practically) original form. (A few more "experiments" were only rubbish). They were written at the beginning of a peculiar period, not mystical but, rather, psychical. I have added some from another, later group (calling it "post" and the other "ante"). The essence of the development in between consisted in the discovery that "hypnogogisms", i.e. the brief visions and auditions between waking and sleeping which many people get are, or can be, clairvoyant. The section "hypnos" is some of the raw material run together pretty much as it came. I omitted a number of the "post"-group which seemed practically automatic writing. A couple included are put in quotation marks because they were of this type, or almost. Later, in 1939, I started putting together some more pieces ("Centrifuge"). What I included is almost all that I ever did. There were to have been other sections, more dreams etc.

If you use any of this stuff I would prefer to have it called "Prose poems" because practically all were actually written in the *Laconics* style first (not in stanzas though) and then run out as prose.

It is interesting you should have noticed these pieces in *New Directions*. Mr. Laughlin seemed to like them. An acquaintance of mine here recently ran across the book in the public library. She said she "laughed and laughed". The earlier ones owe a good deal to Max Jacob (his poems in prose) and the later ones to Kafka, I think. I shouldn't be surprised to be told *New Directions* got the best ones. (Early in 1932 my interest in surrealism was at its peak).

Speaking (out of turn) of the prose anthology generally, for me, of course, it would seem very odd without a story by Morley Callaghan who is about the only Canadian prose writer I really appreciate. There are a lot of good ones in *Now That April's Here* and *A Native Argosy*.[1] Raymond Knister, too, is supposed to have written some fair prose (I haven't read any of his). I heard something about a story in the *Midland* probably called, I think, "Mist-Green Oats".[2]

Yours sincerely,
W. W. E. Ross

1 Morley Callaghan, *Now That April's Here and Other Stories* (New York: Random House, 1936) and *A Native Argosy* (New York: Scribner's, 1929).

2 Raymond Knister, "Mist-Green Oats," *The Midland*, No. 8 (Aug.-Sept. 1922), 254-76.

16

October 2, 1943

Dear W. W. E. Ross,

I greatly appreciate your sending down to me *Distillates* and *Centrifuge* — and thanks, once more, for your good cooperation with my literary projects. I put off acknowledging the mss. until that period when I could command time adequate to them.

I have chosen the following to include in my proposed prose anthology *Canadian Accent*: "The Spring," "The Boat-Ride," "The Tower," "One Man," "Exhortation," "The Animals All," "The Subtle Odor," "Intrusion," "The Spider," "The Voices," "The Fact," "The Difference," "The Hammer". May I include these under the heading "Distillates"? I much prefer this title to

"Prose Poems". They are, of course, obviously prose poems. "The Boat-Ride" and "Exhortation" particularly are beautiful "pure" poetry. In fact, I marvelled throughout at the rhythm you command. Had you noticed that "Close the Windows" (from *Largo*) is "The Cold Night" from *Centrifuge*?

I think you succeed most beautifully in a most beautiful realm. Where dream begins, where dream ends, of the nature of "hypnogogisms", I know not. But you have subtly communicated. I too appreciate the earthy satire and irony of "The Animals All" and "The Hammer".

Yes, I have a story by Callaghan. I chose "Two Fishermen". The index I sent you was by no means complete. I still can find little or no mature imaginative short-story writing in Canada. But I shall hold up the book no longer. What I have, I think, is good.

Again, my thanks. If you are so moved, do send your writings, from time to time.

Sincerely,
Ralph Gustafson

17

62 Delaware Ave,
Toronto, Canada,
Oct. 11/43.

Dear Mr. Gustafson,—

Thank you for your letter about the "Distillates" pieces which are by the way about the very last things I should until recently have ever expected to be chosen for a volume of popular circulation. It seems that what of one's things get picked out in the long run are not altogether those one thinks people *ought* to like — (though this is true to a considerable extent. If one finds one's own choice not backed by others, one should get very suspicious of it. What I mean is something like the feeling which has led so many Canadian writers in the past to think that real poems should look and sound like Keats) — but the things for which one has oneself a secret predilection.

The heading "Distillates" is o.k. to use. It is the one actually used for a number of years. I noticed recently, I think, that the term "prose poems" had been used by one or two of the French writers and it seemed momentarily desirable as expressing a category between prose and poetry.

Yes, I had noticed the similarity between "Close the Windows" (*Largo*) and "The Cold Night", and I must confess that they both owe something, if not a good deal, to a piece by Paul Eaton Reeve in number one of *The New Act*, January 1932, a "little" magazine which ran two or three numbers and was put out by H.R. Hays and Harold Rosenberg. Mr. Reeve's piece, which is not explicitly spiritistic, is as follows:

Malice: Foreshortened

Silent ... it is the house I spoke about
climbing from my mouth. Its many walls
solidify on every side, and on the other side
of widely opened windows unseen stars
invent for fabulous skies familiar scars.
The lamp is shining where I said it would,
an obedient rug touches our feet ... air in the air to breathe
observes within the room, waiting to be heard,
the sound of trees somewhere outside.
Somewhere a voice speaks .... words
unremembered by the two of us.
You heard my voice; these are my words,
but not that voice. Turn
the handle of our door;
beyond our light .... duration of forgetfulness
of forgotten nights, unknown and starless.
When we leave this room we leave the light.[1]

In May 1932 Mr. Reeve had a piece in *Fifth Floor Window* called "Ode for Fly, Jr." which did not attract my interest to any extent.[2] I have sometimes wondered what Mr. Reeve has done, in all, in the way of writing. *Fifth Floor Window* was got out by H.R. Hays, Harvey N. Foster and Marianne Parker. It ran four numbers, the last May/32. The third number, February 1932 was a surrealist issue, and was probably the first explicit impingement of surrealism in America (I don't count here the Paris little magazines of the "exiles"). It is stated in an *F.F.W.* article — "Super-realist work has been printed in two American magazines, *The Little Review* and *Transition*, both now defunct." *Transition*, revived later, was of course printed in Europe. In the May/32 issue were two of my "distillates" — one from

1 Paul Eaton Reeve, "Malice: Foreshortened," *The New Act*, No. 1 (Jan. 1932), p. 16.

2 Paul Eaton Reeve, "Ode for Fly, Jr.," *Fifth Floor Window*, 1, No. 4 (May 1932), n. pag.

3 W. W. E. Ross, "Example" and "Hypno II," *Fifth Floor Window*, 1, No. 4 (May 1932), n. pag.

4 The first surrealist manifesto was published in 1924 and reprinted in 1929; the second appeared in 1930.

5 "Talk of the Town," *The New Yorker*, (9 Oct. 1943), p. 15.

6 Parker Tyler, "Prelude to Hollywood Dream Suite," *Fifth Floor Window*, 1, No. 4 (May 1932), n. pag., and "Shipshape Climber," *The New Act*, No. 1 (Jan. 1932), p. 23.

7 Horace Gregory, "Hellbabies and Others," *Blues: A Magazine of New Rhythms*, 1, No. 5 (1929), 125-28.

8 Horace Gregory, *Chelsea Rooming House* (New York: Covici, Friede, 1930) and *Poems 1930-1940* (New York: Harcourt, Brace, 1941).

Experiments and a "Hypno".[3] They took also for publication two of the Max Jacob translations, but no further issue appeared. I found the February (surrealist) issue very exciting because of the moment at which it arrived, though I was already acquainted, from Paris, with the surrealist manifesto — or one of them — about 1928 or 1929.[4] I thought you might be interested in these historical notes now that surrealism has become popularized (to its detriment, I suppose) in America. I see by an amusing note in *The New Yorker* that Charles Henri Ford and Parker Tyler are editing one of the current surrealist magazines.[5] There was a piece by Parker Tyler in the May/32 *F.F.W.* issue — a "poetry issue" — and also one in the aforementioned number of *The New Act*.[6] Earlier than this in 1929 or before, Charles Henri Ford edited an interesting magazine called *Blues* which ran at least five numbers because I still have #5. Its full title was *Blues: A Magazine of New Rhythms*, and some of the contents struck me at the time as extraordinary (we laughed at them a good deal) — some of Horace Gregory's first work for example — "Hellbabies and Others" — namely "Advice," "Time and Isidor Lefkowitz" and "Hellbabies".[7] The first two appeared in *Chelsea Rooming House* (1930) but I haven't found "Hellbabies" in his *Poems 1930-1940*[8] in which I found a much more sedate tone than in those first pieces. The omitted piece ("Hellbabies") runs:

Hellbabies

Hellbabies sitting in speakeasies
trying to make a million dollars come to life
out of a shot of gin,
trying to make love again
to a new girl,
trying to get out of the way
of sleep and death.

Hellbabies (another brood)
walking through rain,
electric signboards,
in subways,
at shopwindows
their brains filled with tears
trying to get out of the way
of wives and children
because there are

NO JOBS NO JOBS
no work, only walking.

Maybe god is waiting for
these hellbabies,
surely hell is waiting
for them to come home:
Come home, there will be sweet hell tonight,
always ready.

I finally subscribed to *Blues* (in which Parker Tyler appeared) (Columbus, Mississippi). Some time later, having received no copy, I wrote enquiring and got a letter from the mother of the editor explaining that they (i.e. Ford and Tyler) had gone to Paris.* I wonder whether my subscription money helped them on their way.

Yours sincerely,
W. W. E. Ross

* Perhaps she mentioned only the one. I have forgotten.

18

62 Delaware Ave,
Toronto, Ontario
Dec. 26/43.

Dear Mr. Gustafson,—

There is one little error, which I have just noticed in the "Distillates" mss. from which you selected a number of pieces including one called "The Voices". In that piece I left out some words in typing. Instead of "butterflies they pass from bloom;" it should read "butterflies as they pass from bloom to other bloom;".

I notice that the latest "little magazine" here is one got out by Raymond Souster and associates at an army post on the east coast, called *Direction*.[1]

1 The first issue of *Direction* appeared in November, 1943.

They sent a copy to Morley Callaghan, which I have seen — mostly rather nostalgic writing, by young soldiers who wish they were back at home.

With the season's greetings,

Yours sincerely,
W. W. E. Ross

19

January 4, 1944

Dear Mr Ross,

Many thanks for your two letters. I have tried to answer the first for a long time — but work seemed to intervene. I corrected the error you pointed out in "The Voices" from "Distillates". The typescript is now on its way to England.

I'm enclosing a cheque for your poem, "Falling Water", which I included in my *Little Anthology of Canadian Poets* published by New Directions Press — and have had a copy forwarded to you. I do hope you will like the book. I wish the $2.00 could have been larger — but the book's selling-price is low.

Souster sent me a copy of his new publication *Direction* — though I haven't had time yet to see what it is like. I think Souster's verse itself is interesting. I included some samples in the *Voices* collection.[1]

I was most interested in your notes of the early surrealist printings in America. Charles Henri Ford and Parker Tyler are now editing a magazine called *View* at 1 East 53rd Street, N.Y.C. An interesting publication with more than a dash of sensational. I see the last issue is having trouble with the Postmaster General — some nonsense about nudity of their minotaurs etcetera.[2]

What did you think of Art Smith's Anthology? I did a piece on it for the *Toronto Quarterly*[3] — though being allowed only 2000 words I couldn't extend myself very far.

1 Raymond Souster, "Wild Night", "The Hunter," and "Ersatz," *Voices*, No. 113 (Spring 1943), pp. 38-39.

2 *View* was edited by Charles Henri Ford. Volume 1, No. 1 appeared in September 1940. The magazine was banned from the mails because of issue No. 4 of series III (Dec. 1943), which contained a reproduction of Picasso's "Le

Many thanks for your cooperation in my projects and all best wishes for the New Year.

Sincerely,

[Ralph Gustafson]

Minotaur" (1935) that was considered obscene.

3 Ralph Gustafson, "Anthology and Revaluation," *University of Toronto Quarterly*, 13, No. 2 (Jan. 1944), 229-35.

20

62 Delaware Ave,
Toronto,
June 28/44

Dear Mr. Gustafson,—

The intention of collecting and copying out the numerous pieces in the *Allegro* form — and even an occasional beginning — (with the idea of forwarding them to you) — has long delayed my reply to your last letter. It may be I am no longer very much interested in these pieces, myself.

Thank you for the copy of the *Little Anthology*, and also for the cheque. By the way, this is the first time in nine or ten years that I have made any money out of writing! The *Little Anthology* seemed to me to strike a pretty high level, technically. Everything in it seemed well done, each in its own way.

I saw your review of Smith's Anthology in the *Toronto Quarterly*, and thought it was very fair. His method of deflating the "golden age" group, namely, by finding high values in *earlier* poets, does not seem especially successful to me. The more direct method, that of concentrating on *later* ones appeals to me more perhaps. But, of course, his book had to be complete, historically. To me, Heavysege is outstanding among his own group, and for a long time thereafter, but I don't warm up very much over some of the others.

When one is young his interest in, and feeling about, poetry is like a steady, strong stream; or a continuous glow. Later, it becomes intermittent — in my case at least — though its recurrences may *seem* as vigorous as ever. However the intervals between these recurrences seem, unfortunately, to grow longer and longer. At present I am enjoying (?) an unsually long interval!

I hope that *your* enthusiasm continues undiminished indefinitely.

Yours sincerely,
W. W. E. Ross

21

70 Central Park West
New York City
July 7, 1944

Dear Mr Ross,

Many thanks for your letter. It is good to hear from you always. I am pleased that you liked my small effort for New Directions Press. They did the book well and there have been some excellent reviews — in the *New Yorker, N.Y. Herald Tribune, New Republic*, etc[1] — I am very grateful for your contribution. I wonder if you agree with my word of you (stated in my review of Smith's anthology in the *Quarterly*) — that you define Canada's *northness*? I have felt that all along — and no one else quite captures that cool lucidity and the fresh wonder of Canada's northness as you do.

I am told that my Penguin Anthology has set some sort of record for Canadian verse — 85,000 sold. The collection of contemporary Canadian prose pieces *Canadian Accent*, which I did for Penguin's is now in active production in England. It should appear toward the end of this year. I am now in the pleasant task of correcting proof of my own collection of verse, *Flight Into Darkness*,[2] which Pantheon Books are bringing out mid-September.

This is the extent of my literary efforts these days. A book coming out — but no poetry written for these past several months. Not satisfactory — for I weary of editing and exhaust myself on things other than creative in my work here. As you say, intervals between writing seem to grow longer. But perhaps — to use a cliche but not an excuse — it is the times. At any rate, I hope you are at the *end* of your interval. I should be most interested to see new poems by you. Would their form have changed?

I agree about the older samples in Smith's collection. Perhaps I didnt state myself strongly enough in the *Quarterly* review. I have never been convinced of the necessity — let alone the enjoyment — of dragging up historical pieces

1 Reviews of the *Little Anthology* appeared in *The New Yorker*, 25 March 1944, p. 99, the *New York Herald Tribune*, 9 Jan. 1944, and the *New Republic*, 15 May 1944, p. 689.

2 Ralph Gustafson, *Flight Into Darkness* (New York: Pantheon, 1944).

because they are historical. It's a harmful approach. I wholeheartedly agree with your statement in this month's *Forum*.[3] The poetic habitat is a needful thing for the poet — you cant be a carbon if you have got it. My roots are certainly in the eastern countryside. One day, I shall send you a poem of such recognition.

With warmest good wishes,

Yours sincerely,
Ralph Gustafson

3 W. W. E. Ross, "On National Poetry," *The Canadian Forum*, July 1944, p. 88.

22

62 Delaware Ave,
Toronto, Ont.,
Dec. 1/44.

Dear Mr. Gustafson, —

Thanks very much for the copy of *Tomorrow* with your article on Canadian poetry[1] which needless to say interested me much. Your book *Flight Into Darkness* ought to be out about now. Will it be obtainable commercially here? Eaton's book department pick up some books of poems published in New York but not all by any means. Have you put "Epithalamium" in? Though it was published separately was it not? My present view is that a book even of short pieces ought to have at least one longer piece in it to give it solidity, so to speak.

Yes, you seem to have defined well the qualities of those contemporaries you mentioned in your *University Quarterly* review of Smith's anthology (also in *Tomorrow*) — certainly, interestingly. You may be exaggerating when you say Canada is becoming "aware of" all of them — Pratt of course and perhaps Birney because his *David* sold very well.

Pratt's *Collected Poems* are out here and will, I understand, be issued in New York next spring by Knopf, — not by Macmillan's, his publisher here.[2] I am quite curious about the opinion of the good American critics, and I don't mean William Rose Benet[3] — who went "all out" for Pratt recently. If Pratt is so good as he and E. K. Brown etc. say he is, then, by my standards, he should have interested and stimulated me considerably in the long years since

1 Ralph Gustafson, "Apropos of Canadian Poetry," *Tomorrow* 4, No. 3 (Nov. 1944), 73-74.

2 E. J. Pratt, *Collected Poems* (Toronto: Macmillan, 1944 and New York: Alfred A. Knopf, 1945).

3 William Rose Benet wrote

the introduction to the American edition of Pratt's *Collected Poems* (pp. xi-xv). He had previously reviewed very favourably Pratt's *Brebeuf and His Brethren* (*Saturday Review of Literature*, 16 Oct. 1943, p. 24) and *Still Life and Other Verse* (*Saturday Review of Literature*, 29 April 1944, p. 23).

4 The date refers to the publication of Pratt's first major collection, *Newfoundland Verse*, published by the Ryerson Press.

5 The proposed anthology of work from *Preview* magazine was never published.

6 A.J.M. Smith was awarded a grant from the Rockefeller Foundation in 1945 to work on an anthology of Canadian prose.

1923.[4] The fact is, however, I can name thirty or forty contemporary poets in the U.S.A., England and France who have been more effective in that respect, — and several Canadians too. It may be that some of them were better advertised than E.J. Pratt, I mean in the U.S.A. and England, but that is not the case with the Canadians. Of course, I see the geniality etc in Pratt, but personally, primarily, and so it may be impossible for me to look at his work as a stranger would.

Though I heard from F.R. Scott about a *Preview* "Anthology" and also about a writers' association nothing has been said recently regarding these projects, that is, loudly enough to penetrate our Toronto intellectual darkness.[5]

When Smith's two year grant starts next fall I think he's going to spend a few months here, something we and our friends are looking forward to.[6]

It is always interesting to me to note that Marianne Moore and E.E. Cummings are still going strong. It was these two who, in 1924-26 really excited me most keenly among contemporary poets (though I was already acquainted with Lindsay, Frost, Pound (a little), Amy Lowell and Sandburg, not to mention the Untermeyers and Sara Teasdale!). To tell the truth I don't find Cummings very exciting now and have difficulty in accepting that early feeling! Since that time, of course, American poetry has come pretty much under English influence, by way of Eliot at first I suppose. I wonder if Auden will become an American poet and reverse this trend!

I am looking forward to seeing some day the poem you mentioned in your July 7 letter.

Yours sincerely,
W.W.E. Ross

23

New York City
January 25, 1945

Dear W.W.E. Ross,

Many thanks for your letter of over a month ago — which has gone too long unanswered. I was glad that you thought my definition (in the article in

Tomorrow) of certain of the Cdn contemporaries apt. I really cannot think of your work without "northness" in it — and I may add that that has been a pivot of my definition of Cdn poetry as distinct from other. I have been puzzled long now when asked for such a definition down here. It seems to me (reading through the new younger anthology *Unit of 5*)[1] that my ground has become unsteadier. Their work is, in great part, anonymous. Souster has personal passion — but the others might be the work of a hundred others who appear down in here in the little magazines. Dudek is narcissistic; Page likens everything to everything else and seems incapable of poetic *statement*; Hambleton is cerebration that has now become cliche. Chiselled lyricism seems incapable of sprouting in Cdn soil.

I was talking to Patrick Anderson and A.J.M. Smith recently and they tell me that the *Preview* anthology is to be put out by Ryerson. I hope you are adequately represented?

I have done little writing recently — but have had the interest of watching my own book *Flight Into Darkness* unfold in various quarters. It has gone well which is the main thing. I have seen only two Cdn reviews — one in the *Toronto Star* which I liked; the other — a stupid piece in the *Cdn Forum* misreading and misquoting.[2] I was interested in a review that appeared in the *N.Y. Herald Tribune*.[3] It touches on your theme of regionalism and deplores my "lack" of it. Of course I dont lack it. The review is a good example of the pre-conceived notion school. Koch (who's Norman MacLeod's wife) conveniently ignores much in my book that would undercut her thesis — a not uncommon critical practice down here. I'll enclose a copy. Perhaps you might like to read it. Yes. I included "Epithalamium in Time of War" (a piece, by the way, so regional it is full of place-names!) — and agree that a long poem is a fulcrum and a test. There are few out of Canada that are not verbose, garrulous, or unformed.

My prose collection *Canadian Accent* should be out in England though I havent seen a copy. I expect it will be done also in Toronto if I ever can get the publishers moving. I cabled London this week about it.

Best wishes — and I trust you are writing?

> Sincerely,
> Ralph Gustafson

1 *Unit of Five* (see note to letter #10) contained poetry by Hambleton, Souster, Dudek, Page, and James Wreford.

2 Reviews of *Flight Into Darkness* appeared in *The Canadian Forum*, Dec. 1944, p. 216, and the *Toronto Daily Star*, 30 Dec. 1944, p. 26.

3 Vivienne Koch, "Young Canadian's Poems," *New York Herald Tribune*, 7 Jan. 1945, Sec. 6, p. 12.

62 Delaware Ave.,
Toronto, April 6/45.

Dear Mr. Gustafson, —

Thank you for sending me the *Herald Tribune* review of your book. I shall be able to comment on the review and also on poems I hadn't seen before because I secured a copy of the book sometime ago from Jonathan Davie Company, although I saw it in Eaton's later and had probably overlooked it the first time I tried to find it there. Your poems do show a really notable lyrical impulse, something generally lacking now in a pure, authentic form. That is what I've liked about them right along. Their effect depends to a considerable extent on the way you use the word "sun" i.e. frequently and dynamically, not frequently and flatly, as a matter of routine, like e.g. 'death' in the early Elizabeth Barrett Browning. Of course 'love' and 'death' are often the most frequent words in lyrical verse, certainly in the 19th century, but seldom used with any freshness. (It is an interesting point that while Tennyson's most frequent word — in 29 pages from his collected works — is 'death' the second most frequent is not 'love' but 'gold' (Peak period of British commercial prosperity?)) Of the poems I had not seen before, "Flight into Darkness" impressed me, especially from 'And yet, coming on sun across' to the end. Also, the end of 'Myths' — 'Half turned / To her, he heard' etc.

As for the *Herald Tribune* review, I have been vaguely puzzled by it for a long time, when I felt it difficult to write about [it], but now I realize what confused me — simply the fact that — on its negative side — it is pointless, beginning with its main argument. (At a pointless argument I can only gape for the time being). In dealing with a book whose main "setting" is obviously the North Eastern North American countryside — I should say 'farmland' — the reviewer accuses it of 'placelessness' because she cannot make out in what city exists the park of 'In the Park'!

And I think it is pointless to group Hopkins with Eliot, Auden etc. I find little relationship between Hopkins and the somewhat dismal tone of the others, — including MacNeice — and I could say the same about your own poems. Hopkins was not belatedly brought to the front because of any kinship to Eliot, Auden & Coy. but because of his flaring lyricism which filled a vacuum (abhorred by nature!). Not that I don't admire Eliot's poems, at least the earlier ones, but a little Eliot goes a long way.

I, too, was disappointed in *Unit of 5* and especially in Souster of whom I had high expectations or at least hopes. His pieces may have been outstanding in *Unit of 5* but that isn't saying much!

Isn't the *Preview* anthology limited to actual contributors? At any rate I'm not in it. They did go outside their ranks in asking Morley Callaghan who meets them a lot when in Montreal, for a prose piece on the Canadian situation — but I don't think he ever wrote it.

I'd like to see a copy of *Canadian Accent* to find out just what's in it. Will it be on sale this side of the Atlantic, do you think?

I'm glad to hear your book has gone well in the U.S.A. That doesn't happen very often to a book by a Canadian. Smith, Klein and D. Livesay have plunged across the border recently and I'd like to have full reports on their critical reception.[1] One review I saw treated Smith rather lightly (unjustly so).[2] But wait for our immortal Ned's New York appearance, scheduled for the spring. I venture to predict that the collected works of E.J. Pratt will make poetic history in the U.S.A.!

Yours sincerely,
W.W.E. Ross

25

New York, N.Y.
June 10, 1945

Dear Mr Ross,

Many thanks for your letter of last April. The long silence on my part since then is no indication of my appreciation. I was grateful for your remarks on my own poems — especially as printed criticism these days is so often ego-centric and often egregiously inapt. I was particularly struck by your remark on the use I seem to make of "sun". One other person has commented on this use. But until you pointed it out I was not aware that the word was such a lyrical pivot. You're right. I am doubtful whether I should give this any investigation. Sun if anything is spontaneous, and I am inclined to hazard the danger of over-use. At least, I am sure I wont be caught making invocations to it. I dislike invocations to anything — though the use of "O" can be a fine emotional crux.

1 A.J.M. Smith, A.M. Klein, and Dorothy Livesay had all published books in 1944 (the American edition of Smith's *News of the Phoenix*, Klein's *The Hitleriad* and *Poems*, and Livesay's *Day and Night*). Ross is probably referring to American reviews of these books, all of which (excluding *Day and Night*) were published in the States.

2 The review of A.J.M. Smith referred to is probably that of *News of the Phoenix* in *The New Republic*, 8 May 1944, p. 634, or in *Poetry* [Chicago], 65, No. 3 (Dec. 1944), 157-60.

There is probably significance somewhere in the fact that my most considered notices have not come out of Canada. By and large, Canadian notices have been purblind. Not because of praise, or lack of it, of course, but because our reviewers apparently cant read. The one exception is B.K. Sandwell. E.K. Brown's estimation in the *Toronto Quarterly*, I felt, [was] miserly and contradictory.[1] "Smiling charm" is damning. He had previously used "a kind of daintiness" in contrasting my work from Hopkins. Either Brown is passionless himself, or I have notably failed in communication. His charge that I lack music, I must reject out of hand — and if he finds me "difficult" it is because he has not heard my meaning. But then, others have said the opposite. And it is amusing, now that a large part of the field is in, to find that each critic's favourite is different!

Allen Lane, head of Penguin Books, has been here from London. He has asked me to do a follow-up to *Canadian Accent* — and perhaps evolve an annual round-up of Canadian writing. I of course made the deal. It means a unique international outlet for Cdn writers. The American edition of the current *Cdn Accent* is now in the publishing mills in Toronto, and it should appear this year.[2] I hope you will like it.

Meanwhile, I am sending along a cheque for $4.00 in payment for "Distillates". The amount should be much higher — but I could not control other economics.

With many thanks for your cooperation with *Cdn Accent*, and all best wishes.

Sincerely,
Ralph Gustafson

1 B.K. Sandwell's review of *Flight Into Darkness* was in *Saturday Night*, 3 Feb. 1945, p. 14, and E. K. Brown's in the *University of Toronto Quarterly*, 14, No. 3 (April 1945), 263.

2 No North American edition of *Canadian Accent* was published. A follow-up volume entitled *Canadian Accent* II was compiled by Gustafson, but the book failed to be published.

26

62 Delaware Ave,
Toronto, Dec. 13/45.

Dear Gustafson, —

Canadian Accent — the English edition — has been obtainable here at one of the bookshops, so I got a copy, and I think its standard and interest are rather surprisingly high on the whole. I liked the piece by Raymond Knister very much. I suppose you dug it up in the files of *Midland*? I am glad someone (Dorothy Livesay) is collecting Knister's writing, as I have felt for some time this should be done.[1] Morley Callaghan and I both think that while he can't be blown up into a "big" writer (he didn't write enough) quite a lot of his poetry and some of his prose do show a very marked, distinctive talent. I have always associated some of his poetry with that of Holderlin as to tone etc. Callaghan has a ms. long story of his, "Peaches, peaches" — not very good, though, apparently.[2]

There's a new magazine coming out here — *Reading*. The hopeful editors (Ronald Hambleton etc) expect to print 72 pp. of high grade stuff every month! It seems hopeless.[3] I happened to meet Hambleton at a cocktail party. My name was completely strange to him although we have figured two or three times in the same anthology. So our conversation was extremely brief. I think it was confined, on my part, to "Oh?"

No Canadian or American editions of *Canadian Accent* has [*sic*] appeared here yet, so it has received no attention from local critics. Sinclair Ross seems to me a good writer, Anderson and Miss Page very interesting. Brown's article on Pratt didn't seem to me the strongest thing in it. Mightn't the reader (outlander, that is) ask "What's all the cheering about?". I am afraid I rather agreed with the *Poetry* review of Pratt's collected works.[4]

With best wishes, and the compliments of the season,

Yours sincerely,
W.W..E. Ross

1 Raymond Knister, *Collected Poems of Raymond Knister*, ed. with a memoir by Dorothy Livesay (Toronto: Ryerson, 1949).

2 Raymond Knister, "Peaches, Peaches," in *The First Day of Spring: Stories and Other Prose*, introd. Peter Stevens (Toronto: Univ. of Toronto Press, 1976), pp. 8-57.

3 *Reading*, edited by Ronald Hambleton, Allan Anderson, and Lister Sinclair, appeared in 1946 and lasted for three issues.

4 Winfield Townley Scott, "Poetry and Event," *Poetry* [Chicago], 66, No. 6 (Sept. 1945), 329-34.

27

New York 23, N.Y.
May 13, 1947

Dear Mr Ross,

Just a note to say that you will probably be hearing from J.M. Dent & Sons of Toronto who are doing a Canadian school reader and would like to include your "The Saws Were Shrieking" which they read in my anthology.[1] I took the liberty of giving them your address.

Canadian Accent in a Canadian edition still hangs fire. It is much easier to

1 Ross's "The Saws Were Shrieking" was included in *Proud Procession* (Toronto: Dent, 1947), p. 120.

interest outlanders in Canadian writing apparently than Canadians themselves. But it looks as if a 4th edition of the Poetry Anthology will be scheduled. I want, however, to revise the book. Cut out some mistakes (like Kirkconnell, Benson, Creighton et al) and bring in the newer work of the younger
people. Having introduced a number of the latter in 1942 for the first time, I
now hear criticisms of the anthology for not having included work which was
not written at the time I did the book! — but apart from crystal gazing, there
is much now that I'd like to do to the collection.

Have you been writing recently? I've missed seeing you in any of the
poetic quarters.

With best wishes,

Sincerely,
[Ralph Gustafson]

28

62 Delaware Ave.,
Toronto, July 22/47.

Dear Mr. Gustafson, —

Thank you, rather belatedly, for giving my address to Dent and Sons. They
wrote me and received permission to print the piece in question in their new
reader, which is for Grade VI.

The English edition of *Canadian Accent* was on sale here at one book-
shop, at least — Britnell's, I think — and now more recently at Eaton's. It is
interesting to learn there is a continuing demand for the Poetry Anthology.
The tone of the book as a whole is certainly much less soggy, derivative and
dead-heavy than that of most Canadian collections, and it was evidently no
mistake to under- rather than over-emphasize the earlier writers. I agree
about the "mistakes" as far as you named them, certainly Kirkconnell and
Benson at any rate.

I don't keep in touch with the magazines as I used to and so perhaps I
have missed some of your recent pieces?

My own efforts are becoming more and more limited to finishing up and
arranging what I have on hand (what I want to keep, that is) from the last

twenty years or so. It is a question of bringing out more clearly my main theme, or themes. One such collection has been handed around locally a little and is still under revision. My main theme appears more distinctly in it, I think, than hitherto. This theme cannot be acceptable at the present time since, roughly speaking, it embraces much that is anathema in an age of enlightenment. I am much closer, mentally, to the medicine man than to Diderot. There are certain other considerations as well that tend to deter me from attempting publication at the present time.

It may be partly on this account that my interest in the local literary world is far from breathless. It reached its last peak some years ago when Birney, Anderson, and yourself appeared in the *Forum* etc. Still, I now have a considerable interest in Margaret Avison's work, only it is so hard to get a look at the poems she continues to write. I certainly hope you include her in the anthology revision. She was to have a group in *Poetry* (Chicago) but as I don't see every number I am not sure whether it has yet appeared.[1]

And in the literary world at large, I must confess, I fail to see anything to be excited about. Perhaps this is just old age coming on! The curious career of Auden, reversing Eliot's transatlantic shift, is of some interest, but Auden has always seemed to me to travel too much under Eliot's shadow — not an echo, exactly but something pretty close to it. Dylan Thomas' prose, more than his verse, attracted my attention vividly some time ago. "Existentialism" I find vastly less stimulating than the surrealism etc after the last war.

Birney and Anderson seemed to have flattened out.* I hope *you* will be an example of continued and arresting poetic vigor!

> Yours sincerely,
> W. W. E. Ross
> _____

*A mere impression I hope momentary.

1 Margaret Avison, "Five Poems," *Poetry* [Chicago], 70, No. 6 (Sept. 1947), 318-23. Five poems by Avison were included in *The Penguin Book of Canadian Verse* (Harmondsworth: Penguin, 1958), pp. 212-15.

29 _____

2 West 67th Street
New York 23, N.Y.
March 16, 1952

Dear Mr. Ross,

I was glad to see your poem in the *Canadian Forum*.[1] I always look for your work.

1 W. W. E. Ross, "Narration," *The Canadian Forum*, March 1952, p. 280.

I've had a letter from the Penguin Books Ltd in England stating that Messrs Longmans Green & Co would like to reprint your poem, "The Saws Were Shrieking", from the Anthology I did. Apparently the use is for an anthology which will be published in Australia.[2] I have written Penguin's your address and no doubt you will be hearing from Longmans Green & Co in due course.

All best wishes. Can we look for another book from you?

Yours sincerely,
Ralph Gustafson

2 I have been unable to identify this anthology, and Longmans (Australia) could provide no information about it.

30

62 Delaware Avenue,
Toronto, Ontario,
April 24th, 1952.

Dear Mr. Gustafson:

Thank you for your letter of March 16th. I realize I have been feeling some curiosity about several points — whether, for example, there was another (fourth, revised) edition of your anthology of Canadian poetry; whether *Canadian Accent* was ever issued in Canada, or in the U.S.A.; and did Appleton bring out that *Canadian Pattern*, of which I have heard nothing whatever?[1]

The Australian anthology may be for use in schools. I remember a request for "The Saws Were Shrieking" from Dent some years ago. That was for a grade VI book which I have not seen. Then last year brought another request from Dent, this time for a "secondary school anthology" (which I have not encountered).[2] The present query may represent a continuation of the piece's educational career — perhaps grade XII or even XIII!

I like to include something of my own when writing to people, partly because that compels me to finish up pieces, but this time I am not sending anything new, simply a ms. (you don't need to return it) that has been lying around for some time, in one shape or another, — or rather, a carbon copy (not too good) since I type pretty rapidly and have made a number of copies using several carbons. It began when Miss Moore sent a lot of my stuff to Macmillans N.Y. years ago and a reader there drew up a partial list of con-

1 For "Canadian Pattern" see letter #31 and note thereto.

2 The poem was included in J.W. Chalmers and H.T. Coutts, eds., *Prose and Poetry for Canadians: Enjoyment* ([Toronto]: J.M. Dent & Sons (Canada) Limited, 1951), pp. 587-88.

tents for a proposed volume. I didn't have the extra material along the line indicated and let the matter lapse. (It is presumably dead now). Unfortunately, though I have plenty of material now, I dislike the idea of asking any publisher to put money into a losing venture i.e. a book of poems. I would rather publish privately, but that is hardly worth while as one doesn't get any circulation to speak of. Miss Moore mentioned one concern, Twayne Publishers Inc. 42 Broadway. Do you know anything about them or their attitude?

Have you been accumulating material for a second volume? I hope you have. Art Smith said when he had his book published he considered it his final effort. I have an idea one should be careful to keep a lot of material in reserve, even if [it] is merely intended to be dug up, neatly arranged, after one is dead! Publication is so much easier then!

Yours sincerely,
W. W. E. Ross

31

2 West 67th Street
New York 23, N.Y.
May 19, 1952

Dear Mr Ross,

Do please forgive me for not replying sooner and telling you how delighted I was to have *Fresh Woods*. I look forward to reading it and, I know, with great pleasure — for the one or two poems I immediately dipped into brought back to me all the freshness and spirit of your earlier volumes. I hope you follow up with Macmillan's. I personally am not so considerate of publishers (in the light of what they perpetrate continuously) as to consider that a book of poems in a publishers' hands might not cover their costs! As far as I know, Twayne Publishers are quite legitimate and their list of books of poetry are quality (non-reactionary, non-commercial) — though I have had no personal connection with the firm. Had you thought of trying the "Indian File" series of McClelland & Stewart in Toronto?

No, the anthology I did of Cdn poetry stopped with the exhaustion of the 3rd edition. I had a request to revise and bring it out again, and am willing, but it is almost impossible to get *Canadian* distributors interested in the project. *Canadian Accent* appeared everywhere except Canada and the U.S.! "Canadian Pattern" appeared under the title of *A Pocketful of Canada*.[1]

I've now about ready a second collection of poems and would like to see it out. Just as soon as I have a book of my short stories launched, I shall try to hawk the poems!

All best wishes, and warmest thanks, again, for letting me have a copy of your ms — I'm most glad to have it on my shelves.

Sincerely,
Ralph Gustafson

1 John D. Robins, ed., *A Pocketful of Canada* (Toronto: Collins, 1946).

32

2 West 67 St
New York 23
May 7, 1956

Dear Mr. Ross

The enclosed reached me this morning and I thought you would like to have the pleasant request.[1]

It looks as if I shall be doing a revised Penguin anthology this summer and I look forward to including your work again if I may — I shall write you about this.

It was so pleasant meeting you and Mrs Ross at Kingston — though too briefly.[2]

Sincerely
Ralph Gustafson

1 Ross has noted on the letter that this request was from Oxford [University Press].

2 Gustafson refers here to the Canadian Writers' Conference which was held at Queen's University in Kingston, Ontario from 28-31 July 1955. The proceedings were edited by George Whalley and published as *Writing in Canada: Proceedings of the Canadian Writers' Conference, Queen's University, 28-31 July, 1955*, with an introduction by F. R. Scott (Toronto: Macmillan of Canada, 1956).

33

62 Delaware Ave.,
Toronto, Ontario,
May 10/56.

Dear Mr. Gustafson,

Thank you for forwarding the request from James Bulton of London University Institute of Education. I have written him. You may of course include anything of mine in the revised Penguin Anthology. Personally, just now I find Jay MacPherson and Daryl Hine *fascinating* (though I confess the latter's pieces aren't yet what I might call 'clear' to me). I've always liked Margaret Avison's poems too though I haven't seen much by her recently.

We were both (Mrs. Ross and I) very glad to meet you at Kingston last summer. I'm afraid I skimped my convention duties and went swimming instead, though I did gather that publishers are poverty-ridden, and quite unable to publish poetry, although they would like so much to do so.

John Sutherland (*Northern Review*) and his wife have been in this city for a year or so, and we see them quite often.[1] He has been ill but will probably renew the magazine after some months' lapse. A newcomer, presumably to appear this fall, is *Tamarack* (Anne Wilkinson and others).[2]

I hope you will be getting out another book of your poems soon. (You haven't actually done so, have you? — one that I've missed through my present failure — which I must correct — to see magazines etc).

Yours sincerely,
W.W.E. Ross

1 John Sutherland, then the editor of the *Northern Review*, had moved from Montreal to Toronto with his wife Audrey in late 1954 or early 1955, in order to study at St. Michael's College.

2 The first issue of *The Tamarack Review* was dated Autumn 1956. The editors were Kildare Dobbs, Millar MacLure, Ivon Owen, William Toye, Robert Weaver, and Anne Wilkinson.

34

2 West 67 St.
New York
May 17/56

Dear Mr. Ross —

Many thanks for your permission. As soon as I get at the text of the ms. I'll be in touch with you.

I have a book of poems in ms. — but nothing published except a few magazine appearances since I started (to try) to write my novel.[1] The novel is almost finished (abandoned, that is) and I don't know at this point whether I have something — or a failure. If the latter — it will be solely poetry for me — so much more satisfying (and easier).

All best wishes to you & Mrs Ross,

Sincerely
Ralph Gustafson

1   "No Music in the Nightingale," an unpublished novel.

35

Sept. 18, 1956

Dear Eustace,

I have been re-reading all the poems I have of you for the revised Anthology I am doing for Penguin Books. I find I have no less than 14 titles jotted down out of *Fresh Woods* alone. But I have no space to do what I like (Though I have succeeded in bringing the publisher to an agreement for a 256-page book). The "north" poems of yours retain all their fresh, instant, Canadian feeling. I have long meant to ask you — what spot of Ontario did they spring from? For my book, I want this northness — and have again included "The Walk," "Fish," "The Diver," "The Saws Were Shrieking" (the poems contain much more than "northness", of course). I have added a poem of yours I once found in *The Dial*

In the ravine   I stood etc.

If I may use it, shall I title it "In the Ravine"? I have also added "Incident"
and what I think is your best sonnet *qua* sonnet: "Blindness".

Is it all right for me to use this group?

Have I all your work, I wonder? I saw the poems in the *Northern
Review*.[1] Are you writing any? A book of yours should be generally
available — along the lines of *Fresh Woods* — the latter leaves out some that
should be in. Ryerson's should do a volume of yours. Has it crossed your
mind?

I was shocked by John Sutherland's sudden death — at least, I had no idea
he was seriously ill.[2] Though I parted company with NR when it became a
tract, he did an admirable job with it for Canada. I see there is a new Cdn little mag called *Yes* — out of Montreal under the aegis — though not the
editorship — of Layton & Dudek.[3]

I have now been able to emphasize the older Cdn poets in my new
anthology — I was almost entirely concerned in the earlier version with giving the contemporary work a hearing — hardly any had been given up to that
time. Thus, I have got a lot of Heavysege in, some Sangster, two from
McLachlan, Mair, and a better group of Crawford and Cameron. I still avoid
"the historical" — working on the principle, there is no such thing as an old
poem.

I still have to cull and prune, but I think the collection will be what I
hope. I don't really like editing — but this means an international audience.

With all best wishes to you and Mrs. Ross.

Sincerely,
Ralph Gustafson

1 The following poems by Ross
   were published in the *North-
   ern Review*: "The Summons,"
   "Visitant," "Glimpse," "The
   Creek," "View," and "The
   Spring" in 4, No. 4 (April-
   May 1951), 6-11; "The Snake
   Trying" in 7, No. 2 (Spring
   1955), 27; and "Hart House
   Theatre" in 7, No. 4
   (Summer 1956), 20.

2 John Sutherland died on 1
   Sept. 1956.

3 The first issue of *Yes* was
   dated April 1956. It was edited
   by Michael Gnarowski, John
   Lachs, and Glen Siebrasse,
   and published in Montreal.

62 Delaware Avenue,
Toronto, Ontario,
Sept. 23-1956.

Dear Ralph,

You may of course put in the revised anthology the pieces of mine you mention, including "In the Ravine". (I find that title on my own copy.)

Any "north" poems are I think based on two summers' surveying in New Ontario when I was a student. I was a chainman. The first summer we left the C.P.R. main line at Kapuskasing, northwest of Sudbury, travelling by canoe. This was 1912, and I have noted with some interest that it was the year before, in 1911, that Tom Thomson made what was apparently his first canoe trip, with William Broadhead, (before he went to Algonquin Park), leaving the railway at the same point, Kapuskasing. He seems to have made his first serious sketches on that trip. The second summer we were north of Lake Superior, near Port Arthur.

My own "Canadian" feeling was most intense in the twenties, before the declaration of Westminster. Practically all the first section of that book *Laconics* was written one night in April, 1928, after an evening's discussion of Canadian nationalism with friends of ours. The laconics form was developed in 1925 in an attempt to find one that would be "native" and yet not "free verse," one that would be unrhymed and yet definitely a "form". It never "clicked" so well before or since as that night in 1928.

Of course, other elements enter into these "north" pieces. I was brought up in Pembroke on the Ottawa river. The Laurentian plateau begins as mountains along the north shore and we "camped" at Petawawa in the summer. "The Saws Were Shrieking" results from working in a saw-mill during my last high school vacation.

"Incident" occurred on the first surveying trip. The Englishman, the other chainman, was Lemon by name — and it suited him. He was much older than I and had taught school in England. As a marksman he took the lowest possible score. One morning, out on the line, we spotted a partridge-like fowl on a low branch. Lemon, who always carried this newly won pistol, took several shots at it, going closer and closer, and finally hit it on the head with a stick. All the shots had missed and the thing was too stupid to move!

No, you haven't all my work by any means, but the final going over is sometimes delayed for many years. I divert myself from time to time making up little collections — an inducement to do this final going over. I added about a dozen pieces to one such group,* put together recently, and enclose the whole. One, "The Snake Trying", you may have seen in *Northern Review*.[1] I put the more "north" ones at the front. They are of all ages, a very few only two or three years old.

John Sutherland, whom we miss very much, (They had been two years in Toronto.) made a selection of my pieces when he was still in Montreal and submitted it — with my permission — to Ryerson's. Dr. Pierce had expressed interest. John wrote an introductory essay. I have had no correspondence with Ryerson's but John did have and I gather from what he told me that the salesmen nearly faint when a poetry book is mentioned. The last word (as always) was "maybe next year". This collection, intended by John as a "first" book, leaned heavily on the laconics. Ryerson's brought out John's book of criticism (E.J. Pratt) in time for him to see it. Pierce was very kind. Audrey, John's wife, will not destroy any of his papers, which I don't think she has gone over yet. He wrote quite a lot of verse, though not latterly. I don't know anything about it — except one piece on Pratt in *Queen's Quarterly* recently — but think it ought to [be] examined at some time or other.[2]

John had been ill for about a year, in Weston sanitorium for a time, then allowed home last spring, and finally sent to hospital here in June. The original diagnosis was tuberculosis of the kidney, which had laid him up years ago as a student, for three years. One kidney was removed this year. There was really a cancerous condition, and this was the diagnosis after the operation — though not necessarily a highly malignant type. It struck him drastically, however, in June and he spent the rest of his time in hospital, in a stryker frame, paralysed from the waist down. He was his old self, though, at least until the last time we saw him. I consider the loss of John Sutherland a really serious one. Audrey is here for the time being but will probably go eventually to Montreal where she has more friends.

The only way to avoid the historical may be an alphabetical arrangement, or one by subjects. Rand tried the former but his choices were none too good.[3] *Songs of the Great Dominion* used to interest me when I was quite young.[4] Heavysege was my favorite then, and since. I remember speaking to Art Smith about him before Art brought out his collection. I found him curiously fascinating, somehow. Isabella Crawford, too, attracted my attention to some extent. I hope you don't overweight the first part of the revised anthology or too much change its distinctive tone by increasing representation of the older writers. In any case I am sure you will make a good job of it. Some

* I have several copies.

1 See note 1 to letter #35.

2 The collection of Ross' poems was never issued, but Sutherland's introduction is contained in his *Essays, Controversies and Poems*, ed. Miriam Waddington (Toronto: McClelland and Stewart, 1972), pp. 162-64. Sutherland's book on Pratt is *The Poetry of E.J. Pratt: A New Interpretation* (Toronto: Ryerson, 1956). The poem referred to is "E.J. Pratt," *Queen's Quarterly*, 63, No. 2 (Summer 1956), [247].

3 Theodore H. Rand, ed., *A Treasury of Canadian Verse* (Toronto: William Briggs / London: J.M. Dent & Co., 1900).

4 William Douw Lighthall, ed., *Songs of the Great Dominion: Voices from the Forests and Waters, the Settlements and Cities of Canada* (London: Walter Scott, 1889).

5 Oscar Williams, ed., *A Little Treasury of Modern Poetry, English & American* (New York: Scribner's, 1946). Ralph Gustafson recalls Oscar Williams remarking to him that the reason he had never included Canadian poetry in his anthologies was that his own poetry had never been published in a Canadian anthology.

time perhaps Canadians will appear in an international anthology, like Oscar Williams' *Treasury of Modern Poetry*, which is purely Anglo-American — or at least was so in the 1946 edition;[5] and this is as likely to result from your Penguin books as from anything else.

Thank you for your letter which has rearoused my interest in Canadian poetry as Canadian.

With best wishes,

Yours sincerely,
Eustace Ross

37

2 West 67th Street
New York 23, N.Y.
Sept 29, 1956

Dear Eustace,

Many thanks for sending me *Some More Pieces* (which I am keeping for my shelf, if I may) and your letter. I found many poems which I think represent you — as a matter of fact, I jotted down 9 titles in my reading with anthology in mind. I have put in "Culvert" in the place of "Blindness" — I hate to miss the sonnet but have no space — I have so many sonnets out of the poets so far — and "Culvert" does group better — an excellent poem. I particularly like "Butterfly", and then "The Great Blue Heron", "The Snake Trying", "Narcissus", "Rainbow", "Sphere", "Dowsing". Also "Observatory" which should be in Art Smith's and Frank Scott's proposed collection of Canadian satirical poems. The latter has been in the works some time — Frank told me about it last year — but whether it has been gone ahead with, I don't know.[1]

I have an instinctive dislike in scattering poems for an anthology — like Birney's *20th C. Cdn. Poetry*,[2] or any of Oscar Williams — I like a poet to be together with himself — and I don't read poems to fit *my* mood. Alphabets and/or anonymity irritate me — the result of the guessing game is (when you spot it) to be left with the feeling, My what a good boy am I. A man's work stands around his personality and together — or nothing. That's why a series of one-poem-per-poet-anthology is unsatisfactory — though better than *no*

1 F.R. Scott and A.J.M. Smith, eds., *The Blasted Pine: An Anthology of Satire, Invective and Disrespective Verse Chiefly by Canadian Writers*, Preface by David L. Thomson (Toronto: Macmillan of Canada, 1957).

2 Earle Birney, ed., *Twentieth Century Canadian Poetry: An*

poetry. The real job, it seems to me, is a thorough job — of delicate balances and counterweighting and fairness to poet, historical continuity with a good perspective on the how of the development of a nation's poetry — and overriding the whole business, the principle that there is no such animal as an old poem.

I have increased representation of the older writers — but I don't think overweighted the first part of the book. In fact, I have restored a balance on my previous anthology. I have given pride of emphasis to Heavysege (2 sonnets; three pieces of *Saul* and two pieces of *Count Filippo* which no one has paid any attention to and which is an astoundingly good play.) Two poems of McLachlan; five of Sangster; excerpts from Mair's *Tecumseh*; a better selection of Crawford. Cameron I have found to be more of a love poet — somewhat in the Donne mood — than I thought. Then, of course, come the poets of the 60s and so on, with a disdainful jump through Pickthall's better poems straight into the moderns. That's a "balance", don't you think?

And it is most satisfying to find Canadian poems Canadian. Except for Emerson and Arnold getting into the act, there is astoundingly little that can't be pointed to, first, as Canadian. Keats, Shelley, Tennyson, do not loom as large as is generally thought. The big boy on us is W.B. Yeats.

But, like Keats, I am not so much of this bloodhound, influence-seeking, professorial editing-school that yelps "See!"[3]

I am glad to have your paragraphs on the "north" that produced the *Laconics*. I envy that one night in 1928. Your Mr. Lemon fascinates me. I confess to having a sly eye on the English readership when I put "Incident" in. One thing. What do you think of making a period a comma:

The lake not far ahead,
A narrowing. etc.

Don't mean to be arrogant — but the two full-stops tripped me rhythmically.

All the best — and many thanks for *Some More Pieces*. Do please send me these collections when you make them ... and I hope you hear from Ryerson's.

Sincerely,
Ralph

Anthology with Introduction and Notes (Toronto: Ryerson, 1953).

3 I have not been able to locate this quotation. Ralph Gustafson has suggested that he may have been paraphrasing Keats rather than quoting him directly.

62 Delaware Avenue,
Toronto, October 1, 1956.

Dear Ralph,

Thank you for your letter. It makes me feel like putting down comments on Canadian poetry to an undue length but I'll confine myself to a few points.

In case, with added space, you are considering using the first Wabanaki song from *Songs of the Great Dominion*[1] ("Now I am left on this lonely island to die") there is, in my copy, an erratum slip reading — Pages 59, 60. Correction: The two Wabanaki songs are translated, not by Charles G. Leland, but by Mrs. Wallace Brown, of Calais, Maine.[2] My copy is 1889, Walter Scott, London. The erratum slip is however not at the front, where they are usually placed, but at the back, at the end of the poetry text, at page 434. Art Smith apparently never saw such a slip. I remember mentioning it to him but forget whether this was before or after the second edition of his collection was published. I thought that if you cared to investigate the matter you would be in a good position, in New York, to do so. There may be some record of Mrs. Brown somewhere. There is no biographical note on Charles G. Leland, or Mrs. Brown, or John Waniente Jocks either (named as translator of the Caughnawaga Song).[3] It seems to me a point of some interest, especially as the language of these translations, or adaptations, is soberer than the poetic style of the time, and it was not, generally speaking, until later that a more sober style became widespread.

Regarding the "Incident" punctuation, I seem to have had a little trouble there in the first place. The ms. reads

The lake not far ahead.
A narrowing — now in the river

I probably cut out the dash because I was scattering them all over at that time. I hadn't thought of a comma after "ahead" but it doesn't seem bad at all. Whatever you like. I was rather relieved to see the sonnet out. All those sonnets in the book make me squirm a little. They were written mostly as exercises, really. In this particular one the inversions bothered me but I never seemed able to eliminate them without imparting a certain flatness to the line in question. I hope the printer doesn't run "Culvert" together. That has happened before ("The Creek", in *Northern Review*). Incidentally, in "Fish",

1 The two "Wabanaki Songs" are in *Songs of the Great Dominion*, pp. 59-60.

2 Charles G. Leland (1824-1903), American journalist and writer. For Mrs. Brown, see letter #40 and note thereto.

3 I have been unable to identify John Waniente Jocks.

your copy is correct. In Smith's second edition 'cool' repeated is an error.[4] Sounds rather silly, I think. Dudek suggested once my submitting a collection for Contact Press and Souster has several times since. I may do something about this though one would naturally regard Contact Press as for the quite young.[5] Sutherland too wanted to bring out a collection (apart from the one he sent to Ryerson's), but he was ill, or getting ill and I didn't follow up the suggestion. I did urge him to try and carry on with *Northern Review*, though. Apart from him I have little interest in any Ryerson's prospect. I was very fond of him and feel, in a way, that anything he did should be brought forward. I do have some interest in making it clear that I was writing actively in the twenties and have put together, tentatively, a *Poems 1923-29*, almost all of which I think you have seen. Looking through it I find only one sonnet, the one called "The Neophytes", corrected a little from the version in the book *Sonnets*, — the same, I think, as in *Fresh Woods*. Marianne Moore particularly liked "Butterfly". "Culvert" and the others like it date from 1954.

In your own pieces, apart from those which have been included in your anthology and Smith's — and the *Little Anthology* — what has stuck in my mind, so to speak, most of all has been, referring to your book *Flight Into Darkness*, the title piece, especially the last stanza; "Mythos", especially the last few lines; some in *Lyrics Unromantic*, number xii for example; "From Sweden"; and "Prelude". If this is of any interest to you. What I remember, that is my own test, I suppose; (I mean, what is *favorably* remembered — one does remember otherwise as well.) Possibly the carrying forward of some writing through generations is a sort of remembering, on a wider scale. Provided I had already, some time before, read everything written by a certain writer, or during a certain period, if I were called upon to make a selection it would almost certainly consist of what struck me as most familiar, that is, what I had best remembered. Perhaps this wouldn't be a very practicable method, generally, since it requires time; but my point, if any, is that this *may* be something like the actual process of literary 'preservation.'

Among the older Canadians, I confess I haven't been able to 'see' Cameron and Sangster. Here I *do* seem to be remeeting Tennyson. I must admit, however, that my acquaintance with them is almost entirely confined to Smith's selections. "Ysolte" (Cameron) seems to me "Maud" (which I haven't read in entirety) and in Sangster I hear the young Tennyson, 'Airy, fairy, Lilian'.[6] In general, though, I think you are right in pointing at Arnold. It may be that you have dug up something by way of a new 'angle' on Sangster as well as Cameron, and I look forward with interest to seeing your selections. In Crawford I find the blank verse curiously dynamic, more interesting

4 In the revised edition of A.J.M. Smith's *Book of Canadian Poetry* (Chicago: Univ. of Chicago Press, 1948), p. 295, Ross's poem "Fish" has the line "in the cool water" repeated incorrectly. In the second instance, "cool" ought to have read "cold."

5 Ross's *Experiment 1923-29* was published as a mimeograph collection in December of 1956. It is the manuscript referred to a little further on.

6 "Airy, fairy Lilian" is the first line of Tennyson's "Lilian," first published in *Poems Chiefly Lyrical* (London: Effingham Wilson, 1830), pp. 3-5.

than that of Mair (or Pratt). Of course, I suppose it is practically impossible to do blank verse really freshly.

As to what you say about the 'balance' of your book, I do rather like the idea of emphasizing Heavysege. When I first saw your collection years ago I was surprised by its 'sharpness', 'cleanness' (I find it hard to write *about* writing, not being in a university). I think its standard is high, technically, that is, when submitted to a line by line scrutiny, as poetry, the highest among Canadian collections, and I really think this is still true. It is hardly fair to subject a book the size of Smith's to this test. As for the other comprehensive collection, the Dudek-Layton one,[7] their criteria were evidently not so 'technical'. The Klein selections in the two books illustrate what I am referring to, more 'concentrated' in yours. In the D-L book I was struck by three pieces I hadn't seen before, Crawford's "The City Tree", Dudek's "The Pomegranite", and Reaney's "Antichrist as a Child". I wrote to Dudek about his piece and in his reply he reported that Marianne Moore had told somebody it was one of the best she had seen for some time. If you can maintain the same standard with increased size you will have done a notable piece of work as an anthologist, I think.

I was trying to recall the Montreal groups in the forties and found myself rather foggy about *Preview*. Was their projected anthology ever published? I don't know just who they were either.

With best wishes from us both,

Yours sincerely,
Eustace Ross

7 Louis Dudek and Irving Layton, eds., *Canadian Poems 1850-1952* (Toronto: Contact, 1952).

39

2 West 67th Street
New York 23, N.Y.
October 10, 1956

Dear Eustace,

Your letters are full of help — I remember long ago you typing out for me poems by Knister — by the way, I seem to have had his birth-date from a letter of his wife as 1900, but I see Livesay in her editing of him gives it as 1899 — I suppose her authority is final...

I'll check on the translation of the Two Wabanaki Songs in *Songs of the Great Dominion* — if I can at the NY Library. I presently have both of them in my anthology. The erratum slip is not in my copy (which is the same date as yours) but if not pasted in could easily have fallen out at some time. Would you know the area of the Wabanaki Indian? and the translation of "moo sarge"?

In your "Incident" I have put in a comma

The lake not far ahead,
A narrowing. Now in the river etc

I hope that is all right with you. I have "Culvert" rightly spaced in couplets and trust the printer doesn't ball things up. It is an amazing thing, how poems meet detail disaster in the printing. I have two sonnets in Rodman's *A New Anthology of Modern Poetry*[1] in the Modern Library and BOTH have errors — one a bad one — "These fantastic in the murk" for "There fantastic in the murk." I suppose no one cares really but the author — but to be published wrongly when one is published at all seems too much. Though that isn't so bad as downright gratuitous editing. I had "For Christ's sake" in my story "The Pigeon" — Ryersons preferred "heaven" to "Christ". Another story — "The Circus" in *Tomorrow* magazine appeared with the first page lopped off![2]

I've checked on "Fish" and I have, correctly, "cool" followed by "cold". I was interested to know "Culvert" dates from '54.

What I like about these pieces of yours is the clean translucence. Simpleness is often mistaken for emptiness and I am still angry about a review somewhere by Livesay who thought my *Lyrics Unromantic* juvenile or some word like that.[3] One must be "smart" I suppose. The quality I like is perhaps in "From Sweden" — to pursue the ones you remembered. A new one is "Quebec Night":

The red logs
Crisp on the outside,
The wood solid, being new,
Are chained to the sleigh.
The runner drags a cleat for the hill up,
And the snow is pleated in the logs,
The snow in the far woods
Falling[4]

1 Selden Rodman, ed., *A New Anthology of Modern Poetry*, rev. ed. (New York: The Modern Library, 1946).

2 "The Pigeon" was reprinted in *A Book of Canadian Stories*, ed. Desmond Pacey (Toronto: Ryerson, 1952), pp. 263-73; "The Circus" appeared in *Tomorrow* 8, No. 8 (April 1949), 21-5.

3 Dorothy Livesay, "[Review of *Flight Into Darkness*]," *Contemporary Verse*, No. 14 (July 1945), pp. 15-16. Livesay writes that certain poems "in themselves would have been enough to make a book, without the rather regrettable section, 'Lyrics Unromantic', which appear juvenile in comparison."

4 "Quebec Night" and "Under" (retitled "The Blue Lake")

were collected in *Rivers
Among Rocks* (Toronto:
McClelland and Stewart,
1960), #42 and #41. The poem
for John Sutherland has not
been published.

The internal rhyme I am aware of — but I think it came right as it fell — do you think so? Another new one, of a piece, is

Under

I see,
Through the white lilies
On their pads
On the blue water,
Still,
Where the water nears the shore,
Down through the clear water,
The stems of the lilies
Deep down, to the mud,
Hanging in the shadow
The black pike

Perhaps I should have called it "Freud".

When I heard the news of John's death, I wrote this. If you think it misses I'll withhold it. When one is so near a poem it is almost impossible to judge that feeling of "Yes. It is right."

For J.S., Dead Too Soon

The hand is still.
He has met
What he believed in.
The sound of sun
Is on the hill.

His hand, that day,
Touched the sun
From me, a gesture
In kind, the last
Of him — the short stay

Of sun where the sun was —
Where we sat
Hot, while the poems
Were read. The moment
Was mortality done. Alas,

He knew! I looked up.
Death, I forgot.
Death is forgot —
Who have from that,
Bread and cup.

The ordinary human gesture of friendship — I wonder if he did know when
he did it during that reading in the room at Kingston? If so, it must have
been a leave-taking.

Sangster, while he was on that holiday with the girls and boys in some
cottage in the Orillia woods, wanting badly to be liked, by the other young
blades was called a dope. I am sure he went out and wrote his sonnet
sequence as a compensation and proof he could do something the other
Lotharios couldn't. I have always been attracted, that is, liked the man for it. I
have included "Yearnings" — which fits into my theory. And with much
affection I have included "Pity's Tear Drop" — an almost impossible statement of Victorian morality with blue lights and faces on the barroom floors.
To me it has the attraction of a Rousseau painting. Cameron I have presented, I think, in a new light — as a sort of Johnne Donne amorist (not in
style) — but in mental approach. It brings him to life, I believe, and lifts him
out of the fight-for-freedom tag with which he's usually labelled in anthologies. Strange that you should also think the blank verse of Crawford curiously
dynamic. I have included the whole of "Curtius" — which is a new approach.
"Malcolm's Katie" is jejune next to it — and over-done. The same, I've
included Roberts' "Marsyas". He never did anything better than those closing
lines. But I haven't over-emphasized the older Canadians. I've junked McGee,
Duvar, Goldsmith, Moodie, Sherman, Dalton, Wetherald, MacDonald,
Clarke — and would like to junk Campbell, though I guess I can't, I have in
"Lazarus" and a wicked sonnet satirizing Lampman, not in his works but got
from his column in *The Globe*. F.G. Scott I like better with a second (and
older) reading. He was valid and not righteous. Heavysege is my big man.
The Dudek-Layton collection, at least for me, while good, fails from their
strained effort to collect what no one else has or would. Birney's is curiously
unsatisfying — as if he were looking for the minor verses to fit his scheme of
moods. Smith, I think, often emphasizes the wrong poem of the right man
and gets excited (strangely) about a new batch of ms. What I mean is, WHY
"Idiedaily" of Carman; and 4-to-5 poems of the new ladies (in his new
anthology) where you have only 4 — and, will you understand? — he's taken 3
old ones of mine. That's stated wrongly. No poem that is, is an "old" poem.
Emphasis and balance is intricate. Maugham has said it all: "There are

doubtless stories by writers of perhaps considerable talent that do not chance to please me. That does not in the least affect their merit. I would never claim that my taste is perfect; all I can claim is that in making a selection as this the anthologist's taste is the only standard."[5]

This is a long letter. If you are still with me, all best wishes.

Sincerely,
Ralph

5 W. Somerset Maugham, "Introduction," in his *Tellers of Tales: 100 Short Stories from the United States, England, France, Russia and Germany* (New York: Doubleday Doran & Company, 1939), pp. xxxviii-xxxix.

40

62 Delaware Avenue,
Toronto, Oct. 16-1956.

Dear Ralph,

This afternoon I went to the reference library of the Toronto public libraries, rather than the university library which still suffers from having been burned out about 1890 (I think) and in any case is weak in North American items (England after all is our mother country.) The reference library has a surprisingly complete list of Canadian (and American) historical etc. publications and sure enough I found a dozen or more on the Wabenaki Indians. We know appallingly little on such matters, I fear, because 'wabenaki' means 'eastern' and the term was applied to all the Indians on the east coast from Nova Scotia to Florida but particularly to those of Quebec (and New Brunswick), Nova Scotia and Maine. There was one book on the language brought out by the 'chief of the Abenaki (same as Wabenaki) Indians' in 1884. He lived at St. Francis, Quebec. I could discover no 'moo sarge' in his vocabulary, which in fact lacked the letter 'r'. I looked also at an article in the *Maine Historical Review*, on the language. It wasn't there either, but the letter 'r' *was* present in that dialect. Most of the words are polysyllabic. There was nothing resembling 'sarge' but this (Maine) article gave only a few words. In the Quebec list, quite large, the only word resembling 'moo' is 'mos' for 'moose'. Perhaps 'my little moose' was a term of endearment? But this is a very wild guess and not put forward seriously. 'Sarge' would hardly mean 'little' in any case. Charles G. Leland was a prominent American literary figure in the eighties etc., educated at Princeton and Heidelburg; born in Philadelphia. He wrote a number of books, and was interested in folklore but this interest was at first European — gypsies, Etruscans, etc. He did later become interested in the native Indians. There is a two volume biography of him and a book on Algonquin legends (not in the Toronto library) is listed. The bibliography does not list his magazine articles, which were probably numerous. In the biography, which is almost certainly in the N.Y. library, the names of two or three people who helped him in collecting Indian material are given. That of Mrs. Wallace Brown is one of these. The Indians in her case were those around Passamaquoddy Bay, and she is described as the wife of an Indian agent, interested in native folklore and 'with the talent to make use of it' (or words to that effect.) As the bay, and Calais, Maine, as well, are right on the border it is not clear whether the Indian agent was Canadian or American — probably the latter however. In my hurried glance over the book I didn't notice whether this point was mentioned. As it is quite likely Leland knew Mrs. Brown personally, and may even have stayed at her house while looking for folklore material, what happened is something like the following, by my guess. The two translations must have appeared in one of Leland's publications, perhaps the book on legends, or else a magazine article, and permission was obtained from his publishers to print them in *Songs of the Great Dominion*. When he saw a copy he told the publisher or Lighthall he had not actually done the translations himself and his disclaimer was noted on an erratum slip put into the remaining copies of that (the only?) printing. The copy in the Toronto library has not this slip, but it is probably an early copy. One could find out by examining the biography to what extent he had actually studied the language, or languages, and whether the actual translating was done by the people who assisted him. An Indian agent's wife might very well be familiar with the language.[1]

So this is a border case in more senses than one, geographical, literary. My erratum slip is not gummed in solidly but along the inner edge only. I think Mrs. Brown's name might be mentioned in a note because it is almost certain she supplied the original material, whether or not she did the actual writing in its final form. Examination of the biography, again, might show whether Leland had ever tried verse in any form. So much for the Wabenaki, or eastern, Indians.

Regarding Raymond Knister, while he was 32 at the time of his death, (Morley Callaghan's statement at the time, and portrait in *Saturday Night*) since the date of drowning was Aug. 29 (*Saturday Night*) he may have been born in 1899 after that date.

In "Incident" the comma after 'ahead' is all right with me. The awkwardness arose from the fact that the word 'narrowing' had to do too much work,

1 Elizabeth Robins Pennell, *Charles Godfrey Leland: A Biography* (Boston and New York: Houghton Mifflin and Company, 1906), II, 235-36: "[Leland] had been further helped [in his Indian studies] by the Rev. Silas T. Rand, missionary among the Micmacs of Hantsport (Nova Scotia), who lent him a large manuscript collection of Micmac tales, and by Mrs. W. Wallace Brown of Calais (Maine), whose husband is agent in charge of the Passamaquoddies, and who has

had therefore unusual opportunities of collecting and verifying Indian lore, as well as the talent to take advantage of them." The book of Leland's to which Ross refers is *The Algonquin Legends* (Boston: Houghton, Mifflin and Company, 1884). The source of the confusion over the translator of the Wabenaki Songs was probably S. T. Rand, who (as Pennell indicates) was a friend of Leland's, and whose help Lighthall acknowledges in a note at the end of *Songs of the Great Dominion*.

2. William Douw Lighthall (1857-1954) published poetry and novels, edited three anthologies of Canadian poetry, and wrote several quasi-philosophical books that were influenced by theosophy. The anthology referred to is *Canadian Poets of the Great War* (Ottawa: Royal Society of Canada, n.d.).

covering several minutes during which the moose and those in the boat felt the shores drawing nearer to them.

The only copies of Rodman's collection I have seen are early ones and I am interested to know your two sonnets were included in the book. You are in some distinguished company there.

You refer to a new anthology of Smith's. If you mean the revision of the *Oxford Book of Canadian Poetry* I didn't expect to have more than about 4 pieces in it because he had named that number — said he was 'starting afresh', whatever that means. He considered putting in a couple of the 'Distillates' but these aren't verse, of course.

There are some interesting points about Lighthall, I noticed today. He was quite a prolific writer, on Canadian historical topics (early) and also on evolution, the 'outer consciousness' etc. Did we have a precursor of Bergson in these parts? He died in 1954 at the age of 97! He brought out a volume of Canadian Poets in the Great War 1914-1918.[2]

I had never before noticed Roberts' "Marsyas" but looked it up. The close *is* impressive.

I like the three poems you included in your letter, am particularly impressed by the one "For J.S., Dead Too Soon". In "Quebec Night" I don't think the internal rhyme is out of place. After all, pleating involves repetition, and I think that in verse every possible implication or suggestion is there in the background whether or not we identify it explicitly. There are one or two points that I'll go into, though I realize that detailed textual comment is a good way to lose friends and uninfluence people, but I always feel an itch to do so regardless. In "For J.S." I wasn't sure what 'touched the sun from me' meant, at first reading. I assume it means he screened the sun off you, but I don't know what other word could be used. I thought of 'warded' but it seems too forthright and heavy. 'Hot' didn't seem just right, and I thought of 'sun-hit' if a heavier word than 'touched' was used, but just now all this seems too blunt, taking away too much from the deftness, delicacy, of effect. So I wind up by suggesting no changes. (But I remember 'He has met' seemed a little abrupt and wondered if 'while' should be put before 'he', replacing the period after 'still' by a semicolon.)

At that time I don't think John expected to die soon. His trouble had always been diagnosed as tuberculosis of the kidney, and he had suffered from it years before. This seemed a recurrence only. It was not until early this year that cancer began to loom up. He had noticed a lump when he went to Weston in the fall of 1955 but the doctors had ignored it. No cancer diagnosis was made until after his operation last spring.

It occurs to me just now — could a ? be put after 'knew' instead of a !? In that case would the 'Alas' indicate regret or sorrow on the writer's part that he *might* have known, instead of at the idea that he *did* know, even then? But I had better leave off. Concentration is confusing me, 'he has met' no longer seems abrupt, as it did the first time, etc!

I guess one can only give one's *first* impressions. In "Under" which, it occurred to me, I would like to have written myself, I noticed 'through' as seeming inaccurate, 'the stems of the lilies' as containing more words than necessary, and the repetition of 'down'. Then it occurred to me 'I have seen' might replace 'I see'. Would that make it more impressive? With respect to the second 'down' however, it seemed that the third last line *should* be kept longer than the very effective — partly *because* shorter and equal? — last two lines. The first two lines would read "I have seen/Below white lilies ... *In* the blue water ...... The lily-stems, ..." leaving avoidance of repetition of 'down' as insoluable since 'Deep, to the mud' would render the last two lines less effective.

In "Quebec Night", my first impressions can be indicated as follows: 'The wood solid, being new,' omitted or changed as not something *seen* (except by looking closely at the ends of the logs); 'for up the hill', since with 'hill up' 'up' tends to become a noun and 'hill' an adjective, unless 'up' remains an adverb in which case it would tend to modify 'drags', both of which seemed to me awkward; 'The snow in far woods/Falling', 'the' seeming superfluous, pointing towards the woods from which the logs came, to be sure, directly, but by implication if omitted. Of course, as usual, on *second* thoughts, after prolonged examination, I wonder, "Isn't 'hill up' OK because bold, somewhat strained, and ending, with difficulty, in 'up'?"

Two of the pieces I enclose are in a style of mine you probably haven't seen anything of, though it protrudes quite a lot. The Merlin piece, from 1942, exemplifies one of my own attempts at that impossible form, blank verse. It is based on prose in Bulfinch. It seemed too even, smooth, 'english'. It arose, I think, from the suggestiveness of 'Brécéliande'[3] and while there is a sort of 'music' running through it, it may be too subdued.

This, too, is a long letter, and something of a hodge-podge.
With best wishes,

Eustace Ross

<hr>

Canadian Forum has taken a series of "Squibs"[4] (about 2/5 of the total), and I am worrying for fear some people will find them offensive. I don't know

3 Brécéliande is the forest where Merlin was enchanted by Viviane. See Bulfinch's *Mythology: The Age of Fable, The Age of Chivalry, Legends of Charlemagne.* (New York: Thomas Y. Crowell Company, 1970), pp. 391-92.

4 For these "squibs," see note 1 to letter #44.

which ones the *Forum* will print. I refused to let Sutherland print the lot. (I also refused to let him print the 'Canto 101', because of Pound's unfortunate situation).

————————————

I remember now I noticed the library copy of *Songs* etc as more ornamental in binding than mine, which is quite plain except for the back, so mine may be a later printing — though it is not so marked — especially as it was not purchased till 1898.

————————————

41

2 West 67th Street
New York 23, N.Y.
January 28, 1957

Dear Eustace,

So many things I'd like to discuss with you — but first my sincere apologies for not answering, thanking you for your last letter. It is only that I kept putting it off because I wished to write so much about it — and then, in between our dates, I have been to England and back.

First your kindness and time about the Wabenaki Indian poems puts me greatly in your debt. If I use the poems I shall look into your points. I say, if I use them, for it strikes me now that I should just simply leave out translations from my Anthology — Red Indian or Eskimo. Having them in sort of strikes me as a hinge that flops in front of the book.[1] All the rest is literary directly, and all the rest neatly means that I have covered a hundred years of Canadian poetry — from Heavysege to Leonard Cohen and one or two other 'youngers'.

I've finished reading texts — books and magazines — the chore is done except Preface and indexing etc. Of course, I find I am left with a much larger book than my publishers will allow! That always happens. So now I shall do the shakedown — cutting the less good poems and (alas) dropping some still good poems. So I shall have to carefully weigh my emphases over, getting all in proportion, and relative. Most of my hard heartedness will be done on the older poets — like my other anthology, the worth it seems to me

1 *The Penguin Book of Canadian Verse* did, in fact, include a "Wabanaki Song" and an "Eskimo Song" (pp. 29-30).

is giving audience and space to the poems living with us and about us. I hope to have a book with not a bad poem in it — but of course that means the impossible, perfect judgement and taste. But the collection will, I think, be clean and concrete and living.

I have been arrogant enough to put some of my own poems in — not 'arrogant' perhaps — perhaps honest enough. Would — out of your memory — the following be all right for me: "Epithalamium in Time of War", "Excelling the Starry Splendour...", "Flight Into Darkness" (with the 5th stanza cut out — Ned Pratt tells me that the poem's last stanza still "haunts" him) — then, in contrast to the verbal texture: the simple "From Sweden" and this:

Incident in Riga

Snug in village sun,
Onion-shape
The steeple, up

Out of dullard sun
In giggling shade
The children hid

Climbed to timbered sun
With pardoned stones
For Jewish ones.

Whistling the schoolboy sun
Did Jacob learn
Hard stone.

O gentle Jesus Son
Whose sweetness then
Did bruise with stone![2]

2. This poem was collected in *Rivers Among Rocks*, poem #35.

I have obtained from Raymond Souster your *Experiment* — and am delighted to have you in collection again. But you must be presented in durable book format. And have a distribution more adequate than I suppose Contact Press is able to supply. The link you supply in Canadian letters must be placed in substantially — I mean, more than an anthology can do.

3 "E.P. in Heaven" is presumably the "Canto 101" mentioned by Ross in the previous letter. The text of the poem is not among the Gustafson Papers.

I loved your parody of Robert Frost — I think it is absolutely first-rate. Chuckled all through it. And I like the "E.P. in Heaven" —[3] though I'd like to see a taughtening here and there in the course of it. I'm grateful for your comments on the new short ones of mine I sent you. I will get at them again in the light of what you say — particularly my one about the pike. Could you send me a copy of the *Forum* with your "squibs" in it? Would like to see them. I've done a series on Cdn poets which I call "Rude Ruminations" some of which are:

Doors and windows
Builded Bliss
But where's the bloody
Edifice?

A swan, a pool, a moth, a star;
A can of Celtic paint
And all the things you think they are,
Ain't.

All the T.N.
T. that is 'll
Never make A.
J.M. sizzle.

One step forward
Two steps back
(Hail Columbia)
And take up slack (Title: "Vancouver Washday")

*   *   *   *

Oiving's
Unnoiving

East of the City

Wadda
Ya mean
He don't like

Choklit
Creams

Louie?
Phooey.

Have you heard of Smith's and Scott's *Blasted Pine?* anthology of
Canadian satirical verse — now being published by Macmillans. Smith's
Oxford Book of Canadian Verse is now also done, I believe.[4]

4 See note 2 to letter #45.

   Saw a detail of a Japanese print in yesterday's *Time's* Book Sections — a
delightful 12th century thing. Don't know what's come over me — now writing Hokkus!

From a Kakuyu Print

The man walks by the flower.
Frogs slap their sides,
The hare rolls with laughter.

Yours,
Ralph

42
---

62 Delaware Avenue,
Toronto, Feb. 6-1957

Dear Ralph,

Thank you for your letter. Regarding the Wabenaki poems, while it is the
case that editors of contemporary or recent anthologies (the contents, I
mean) have usually considered it necessary both in the U.S. and England to
begin with something that doesn't strictly belong — Hopkins or Emily Dick-
inson or Indian stuff — I don't think it would be a bad idea to begin with
Heavysege in a Canadian collection. An earlier writer, if any included, could
be slipped in after, slightly out of chronological order. I don't think this would
be very noticeable?

1 The poems to which Ross refers are "Thaw" and "Quebec Sugarbush," both collected in *Flight Into Darkness*, pp. 74-75 and 40.

Yes, the titles you mention, of your own, are about those that come to my mind first, except that I have always liked the pieces beginning 'Procrastination fumbles/Every frond' and 'So imminent the earth's returning'.[1] Possibly the latter recurs to me more often, it may be because of 'Telesphore of the crimson tuque'. The explanation may be that in the part of Pembroke, Ontario, where I lived there were many French-Canadians — Laplantes, Lafleurs, Poutvins (however you spell it, pronounced Putvah) with Isadore and Telesphore as boys' names. In "Incident in Riga", I always think it advisable to eliminate 'did' if possible. Could it be 'See Jacob learn'? and, simply, 'Bruised with stone'? In that case, however, the line 'Whose sweetness then' would have to be lengthened to three beats, with another word. As it stands, I find 'sweetness' slightly indefinite as to its exact *present* connotation, that is, with reference to the incident, the 'bruising'. If you will pardon this comment, I'm so physical-minded. The 'sweetness' of the 'Son' has now been altered, hardened, transmuted, somehow. 'Whose sweetness, ... then,' with some word which would have to be found, in the space? Just a suggestion, as it appears to me at the moment, perhaps impertinent. (The only word that occurs to me, as worth examining, is 'changeling'.)

This piece is interesting as an example of how one of your 'condensations' looks when spread out a little, showing how it 'ticks'. (If this remark means anything!)

Regarding *Experiment*, the remarks at the end are entirely Souster's. I wanted him to mention Raymond Knister and Dorothy Livesay in referring to American influence in the twenties. (I suppose, Charles Bruce too? I don't know just when A.S. Bourinot, who, I think, was in my year at college, though I didn't know him as I was in science and he in arts, adopted his recent style.)[2]

In "E.P. in Heaven" I think any looseness in the first part was due to my attempt to express tedium. I had already shortened one phrase.

The 'Rude Ruminations' are very neat indeed. I like best "All the T.N." and "Oiving's". I'm not sure I get the import of "Vancouver Washday". What I called "squibs" aren't that, really, but attempts at doing a stanza as various writers *might* have done it — in their off moments, unfortunately, if there was anything to take hold of, any handle. They haven't (i.e. about half of them) appeared in *The Forum* yet and I won't mind much if they don't appear, as I'm afraid people will take umbrage, though they shouldn't. I don't think I would. The stanza, of course, was 'Water, water everywhere'. I rather like the Pope and Dryden ones (where there wasn't much of a 'handle'):

2 Arthur S. Bourinot graduated from the University of Toronto in 1915.

John Dryden.

> The sun but seemed a labourer in vain
> That sucked up needed water while the salt
> Remained behind, a plague, to give us pain,
> Making us fail beneath his fierce assault.

Alexander Pope.

> One thing was lacking in our present state
> Where salt and water mixed contrived our fate;
> The wit to separate them none possessed,
> Without that wit how worthless all the rest!

With somewhat more 'handle':

Bliss Carman.

> In a ship on a stagnant sea
> We awaited a faraway maid
> With a pail of water but she
> Came not and we were afraid.

P.K. Page.

> After the brief voyage we found ourselves stuck
> flies on fly-paper, ship on Sahara sea,
> where no sounds touched the antennae of our ears
> and our throats cried in vain for the ice-cream of the poles.

etc. etc. They were written in 1948, all but about half a dozen.

In a 'ruder' style, I have quite a lot of short pieces, mostly quatrains, and these are accumulating gradually. Examples:

Confession

> Eliot's gloom, distilled and pure,
> Is somewhat difficult to endure
> And so, instead, I turn a lot
> To Auden, the common man's Eliot.

Odd

The curious thing about Irving Layton —
He seems to have a perpetual hate on.

Admiration (Robert Frost again!)

In admiration I am lost
Seeing the skill of Robert Frost.
Fence-essence, the way he hits on it!
What's more, the way he sits on it!

Penalty

From Dante's tour of hell's domain
One fact is easy to retain —
Dante's disapproval meant
Nasty eternal punishment.

Goethe's Salvation of Faust

Faust began in a natural way
With curiosity love and play;
Ended at peace with God and his neighbor
As supervisor of forced labor.

Again the Purple Cow
(Commentary on the cult of the iceberg in Canadian poetry)

I've never seen an iceberg near.
Perhaps I'll never see one.
But this I say — and I'm sincere —
I'd rather see than be one.

and so on, and so on.
  Here's a recent one, in a different tone. (You know the limerick?)

Another Stein

From talented people there's much we can learn:

Ep, Ein and Gert, and now there is Bern.
So drink to their lustre and drink to their health;
To all the Steins honor and comfort and wealth!

I haven't seen Smith's and Scott's satirical collection. I'm told Scott has
brought out a similar collection of his own *The Eye of the Needle* using the
Contact Press name as publisher.[3] I hope these books haven't got that 'Canadian' would-be feeling about them.

I really like and remember clearly "From a Kakuyu Print" (I haven't seen
the *Times*). I don't think a cult of very short pieces harmful as it should help
the writer in longer ones. (I'm continually trying to arrive at ways of con-
structing longer pieces, where real freshness is difficult).

Enough for the present, I think.

Yours sincerely,
Eustace Ross

3 F.R. Scott, *The Eye of the
Needle: Satires, Sorties,
Sundries* (Montreal: Contact,
1957).

P.S. Here's another one just done (I've been checking on *Faust* Part II).

Conclusion of Faust Part II

Satan, master of sly tricks,
Thought he had Faust in a fine fix.
Stunned, when the bargain was deleted,
On end the Devil himself was cheated.

43

2 West 67th Street
New York 23, N.Y.
March 13, 1957

Dear Eustace,

The Anthology as such is done. Your group is: "The Walk", "Fish", "The
Diver", "The Saws Were Shrieking", and "In the Ravine". I as usual was running into space difficulties, but I think this group is fine? I can offer $5.00 a
poem. An elegant sum indeed, but publishers are hard bankers.

This business of copyrights is holding up the ms now. It is endless — and publishers hold one by the nose — besides other vague manoeuvres. I find unmentioned the fact that if a publisher lets a book go out of print, their copyright lapses and reverts to the author. Last time, in my innocence, I paid for Cameron and Crawford — both were long in the public domain.

I liked particularly (again) your take-off on Robert Frost — and again "The Purple Cow". And your squib on P.K. Page. If they come out in the *Forum* please send me a copy if you have one. My "Vancouver Washday" referred to Dorothy Livesay.[1]

Doing an anthology, I find I write only short pieces:

Wagner Unbegrenzt

We took off our shoes in the opera
It was Wagner,
Goetterdaemmerung
(The consonants are what to watch)
So I suppose it was all right
Siegfried set off
In his wife's armour
(That is, his aunt's,
His mother was the daughter
Of his wife's father)
And got a spear in his back
But our two feet were consonant
Yours like a silk cat
Listening to a tuba

All the best,

Ever,
Ralph

_____

1 "Vancouver Washday" parodies lines from the opening section of Dorothy Livesay's "Day and Night," in *Day and Night* (Toronto: Ryerson, 1944), p. 16.

44

62 Delaware Avenue,
Toronto, April 18, 1957.

Dear Ralph,

The April *Canadian Forum* has about 40 per cent of the "Air with Variations" pieces and I have asked them to send you a copy, though I don't suppose anybody will like them very much.[1] They didn't include the one on
Smith (which *he* didn't like years ago — almost all were written in 1948):

A.J.M. Smith

Some said there was water to drink, but most said not.
We had heard one report of the sort; an embittered king
Stinking and salt. He pointed accusing hand
Out over the barren sea, but quickly was shot.

Pieces like "Admiration" and "Again the Purple Cow" were not in this
group, but in another long group entitled "Here and Now".

Still another group is represented by the enclosure, "Remarks". These
number about 100, but not all finished. I seem to have been prompted to try
and counter this 'naive simplicity (or emptiness)' impression that has got
around more or less. Clarity is little understood nowadays after the Richards,
Leavis, Empson et al. campaign.

"News Report from Above" will appear, presumably, in Ray Souster's
new 'little magazine' *Combustion*.[2]

I can't keep track of Art Smith's anthologies, never seem to see them
downtown. You referred a while back to a 'new anthology', but I don't yet
know what you were referring to.

The quarrel, Layton and Dudek against the critics, continues.[3] I sent a
couple of longish pieces bearing on this to Dudek, in letters. I owe him a letter right now, but that is the usual situation, with me.

I had Peter Russell,[4] of *Nine*, send me a lot of English 'little magazines'.
Stand appeals to me most. Do you know it? On the inside of the front cover
of the second issue (mimeographed, later issues printed) appears the following, which I found amusing:

1 W.W.E. Ross, "Air with
Variations," *The Canadian
Forum*, April 1957, p. 22.

2 The first issue of *Combustion*
appeared in January 1957.
Ross's poem, "News Report
from Above," was in No. 3
(July-Sept. 1957), p. 3.

3 See Louis Dudek, "Layton
Now and Then: Our Critical
Assumptions," *Queen's Quarterly*, 63, No. 2 (Summer
1956), [291]-93. Dudek was
writing in response to A.J.M.
Smith's review article, "The
Recent Poetry of Irving Layton: A Major Voice," *Queen's*

Quarterly, 62, No. 4 (Winter 1955-56), [587]-91.

4 Peter Russell was the editor of *Nine*, an English magazine of poetry and criticism which began in 1949. *Stand* was edited by John Silkin and began in 1952. The epigraph which Ross quotes is in issue No. 2 (1952), p. 1.

A critic alleging that the only sensible talking horse in history is the horse Falada, in Grimm's Fairy Tales, forgot the man who hailed a cab in Muncaton in 1867. As he did so the horse turned and said: "Have you read Romola?" and the fare said "No, why?" and the horse said: "I wrote that book in my heart's blood." The fare then said to the cabby: "18, Bladder Place" and got into the cab.

The cabby, who was picking his teeth, said at length: "I like a good book — 'Who killed Paul Ferrol?' that was a good book," and the horse said: "Not so good as Romola. I tore myself to pieces writing that book." The fare said: "18, Bladder Place," and the horse said "I literally dragged that book from the very depths of my being."

The cab then moved off, very slowly.

From "Beyond the Headlines," by Timothy Shy (D.B. Wyndham-Lewis) and reproduced by courtesy of the *News Chronicle*.

Here are some recent odds and ends of my own:

Poisonous

"Who was the black widow I seen you with last night?"
"That weren't no black widow. That was the senate
security sub-committee."

About the second limerick I have attempted:

Beside the Pyramids

"Just look at that lynx! How he slinks
In aversion, away from the sphinx!"
Remarked a pert miss
To her boy, who said this:
"You minx! The lynx thinks the sphinx stinks!"

The following is based on fact to the extent that a mining man here *did* try to browbeat Jack Kent Cooke in his office at *Saturday Night* and was thrown out.

Incident in a Publisher's Office

"You shall not humiliate a humble publisher, Lord Goldenmines," said
J.K.C., "Let me tell you this (remembering G. K. Chesterton): You'll not
succeed by all your wiles of power or the power of your wiles. The evil of
goodness is the goodness of evil. The truth of beauty is the beauty of
truth. The display of triumph is the triumph of display. The height of
ambition is the ambition of height. The editorializing of humility is the
humility of editors. The presentation of news is often the news of presen-
tations. A journal expresses opinions; its opinions express the journal.
The creation of messages is the message of creation. I'd not like you
damned but I'm damned if I like you. I'm surprised by your excitement but
you may be excited by my surprise. The restraint of coolness is the coolness of restraint. So end your warm-up or I'll—

At this moment Lord Goldenmines collapsed from over-yawning.

"You're shamming quitting, so quit shamming!" said the publisher.

Here is a rather ignoble effort:

Feverish, See   J. Yeats Masefield

I must go down to the seas again, to the lonely sea and the sky,
And a small cabin build there, of clay and wattles made;
For all I ask is a tall ship and a star to steer her by,
As I live alone in the bee-loud glade.

And I shall have some peace there, for peace comes dropping slow,
With a wild call and a clear call that may not be denied;
There midnight's all a glimmer, and noon a purple glow;
I must down to the seas again, for the call of the running tide.

Yes, I will arise and go now, for always night and day
The wheels kick and the winds sing and the white sail's shaking,
While I stand on the roadway, or on the pavements gray,
With a gray mist on the sea's face and a gray dawn breaking.

Yes, indeed, I must down to the seas again to the vagrant gipsy life
Where I hear sea water lapping with low sounds by the shore,
To the gull's way and the whale's way where there the wind's like a whet-
                                                                    ted knife;
I hear it in the deep heart's core.

Perhaps this is all you can stand at present?

Yours,
Eustace R.

_____

I keep adding to "Air with Variations". Here's one on Empson:

Mainly, the trouble was we couldn't stay.
Likewise, we found we couldn't get away.
In fact, it seemed to be about this way —
We couldn't go, and yet we couldn't stay.

[The following were enclosed with this letter.]

REMARKS

Poetry

From the spheres was music given.
That is why it speaks of heaven.
Painting remained on earth to glean
Objects scrupulously seen;
And every art has its own place
Adorning it with native grace
Excepting poetry alone
Which in no region has a home.

Perfection

Do not attempt to discover perfection only in Nature,
Human nature as well; the perfect eludes at best.

Descent

If among angles a bright one descended, proud, if unwillingly,
It does not follow that man, too, is an angel by birth.

Cities

Cities are built for men, and for permanence, — such the endeavor, —
For men and for women too; their beauty is fragile at last.

Human Nature

Nature of humans can change, be altered by specious manoeuvres?
Yes, if when time is ripe, blossom comes after the fruit.

Fall Planting

Bulbs stuck into the ground are intended to bring forth glorious
Various flowers of spring; jewels to gladden the eye.
And, as a matter of history, this is the usual sequel, —
Given the name of the seed, certain the shape of the fruit.

Beauties

Beauties here upon earth, as often remarked, are impermanent.
That is to say, for the most; some poems do not fade.

The Chosen

Many indeed are called, but few, it was said, are the chosen.
Here, at least, it is true; in poetry, clearly, this holds.

Truth and Beauty

"Beauty is truth, truth beauty", asserted by some of the poets;
Plato perhaps at the start; Keats, to be sure, of late.
Yes, in this one regard, at least, these two appear similar. —
Beauty made havoc of Troy; truth too's a dangerous thing.

Man's Fate

Satan has never, since, regained the fine figure he forfeited
There in the garden's close, after conversing with Eve.

Curiosity

Angels may skim along over our world's level, eagerly spying.
Perceiving Adam and Eve, do they see the serpent as well?

Wisdom

Wisdom. — The searcher, finally thinking he'd made the discovery,
Found it not pleasant at all; more like an aching tooth.

Power

Power is not what we think it, and often the wielders of power
Act, by choice, in the dark. Rites that are secret are safe.

Tolerance

The ancients respected the mysteries, faith, religion of others.
All but the barbarous then; now too, derisive, some yell.

Appearance

Evil spirits, they say, may assume the bright raiment of angels.
Good angels too may appear, clad in the drabbest hue.

Flags

Red white and blue are the colors most common to flags of the nations;
Red for blood, steadfast blue; white for pureness of motive.

Phoebus

Phoebus, throughout the brilliant day,
Strove to keep the stars away.
Sunk to rest, long after noon,
Out there rushed the stars and moon
Who straight began their nightly play, —
And dispised the loveless day.

1953

Glory of the Dictator

Soaring, the eagle perceives not the world in its marvellous fullness
For he but seeks his prey; seeing, the eagle is blind.

Graceless

How foolish and childish are all unenamored with, heedless of profit!
Grace has passed them by, measured in dollars and cents.

The Flaw

After all gods, higher powers, were ruined by reason, demoted,
The process revealed a flaw; all that remained was God.

Precaution

Fearing lest out of the mouths of babes may come chatter of wisdom,
Into these mouths let's stuff what's fit to stifle that noise.

Dreams?

Is it in dreams or farther that one will, after wandering,
Past the nets of the sea, meet with one's own self?

'They Also Serve'

'They also serve' etcetera. However, among the unblinded,
Those who wait may serve; waiting, they may not be served.

Magic

'Magic' — a loose-tongued term for the far-fetched, nonsensical, fanciful;
Not altogether though; sometimes magic is real.

Matador

Doubtless he's valiant indeed in his nimble eluding of horn-pricks;
But what a complexity here! What intricate killing of beef!

Whom the Gods

'Whom the gods love die young' was a saying approved by the ancients.
They 'kill the thing they love'? No, this is not the case.

Peace

Peace may come and be permanent, after the time of mad quarreling,
Once each side ignores the fact that it alone's right.

Black and White

One current they say is white, while black marks another, contrasting.
Sunlight on ripples is bright; the dark is the gaps between.

To Zimmern   Holderlin
(translated from the German)

The lines of life are different, as are roads
And the mountains' contours. What we are here, a god
Can there complete, with harmonies,
Eternal recompense, and peace.   1937

Final Reply of the Delphic Oracle
(Purportedly in the Emperor Julian's Time)
(translated from the late Greek)

Say to the king: The cunning-built
                hall now lies on the ground.
No more does Phoebus possess
                a cell, or laurelled diviner,
Or babbling spring, and now
                the talkative water's departed.

                                        W. W. E. R.

1957 — except where marked otherwise

News Report from Above

We arrived before the pearly gates.
Waiting outside was Butler Yeats.
"They won't let me in today," he said,
"I've got to bone up on religious ed.

"It seems I'm short on theology;
Disparaged a central authority.
I failed to follow the stalinist line;
Had little notion of the divine,

"Unable to care and not to care
For painless pain and prayerless prayer,
For emotion that is emotionless,
Conclusion that is conclusionless.

"Lacking a truly scholarly tact
I mixed up the motion with the act;
Tried, like Peer Gynt, to be myself.
An error. It's put me on the shelf!"

A flutterless fluttering in the sky.
Mr. Eliot came gliding by.
Suavely alighted, and rang the bell.
He knew the password. He'd learned it well.

The gates opened rather gingerly
Until they were certain that it was he
When a rollicking, welcoming shout was heard.
In popped Eliot like a bird.

A tone of command, like a warning, rang.
The pearly gates shut to with a bang.
Outside in the cold and darkness waits
Unwillingly William Butler Yeats.

W. W. E. R.
1956

45

2 West 67 St
New York 23, N.Y.
April 22, 1957

Dear Eustace,

I've got in my Bio Note on you: Geophysicist with the Agincourt Magnetic Observatory near Toronto. Is that right?

Many thanks for your letter — grateful to have "Remarks" — and I'll look forward to the issue of *Cdn Forum* with your "Air with Variations". I suppose I should subscribe to the *Cdn Forum* — a lot of good new poetry in it — as formerly? What do you think of *Tamarack*? Format's good if they can keep it up. I suppose they pay? It may establish itself. Ray Souster is sending me his *Combustion*. Would like to know about Dudek and Layton's quarrel with the critics. Where is it being printed — letters to the papers? I suppose it's about Ryerson not carrying *The Improve Binoculars*?[1] A grand book, by the way. Good poetry in it.

I don't know the English little magazines — nor *Stand*. There's a new one down here called the *Evergreen Review* takes poetry and short stories and is put out by Grove press, 795 Broadway, New York City 3.

Art Smith's anthology is a English-French one called *The Oxford Book of Canadian Verse*. The Canadian one in their series — Australia and N.Z. have already appeared. I hear also that Art Smith is doing another revision of his *Book of Cdn Poetry* — the big one.[2] And his and Frank Scott's satirical anthology *The Blasted Pine* should be out soon.

What ferment in Canada! I've written my Preface as if we were all established. But does anyone read Canadian poetry — I mean among the Rotarians and on the golf course?

What do the first three lines of "The Plot Against Proteus" mean?[3] I've always liked them — Smith's poem, I mean.

Edelweiss

I try to move you to love by verse.
This is an Alpine movement
Diminishing me
Who should not need
     Hannibal and

1 The first edition of Irving Layton's *The Improved Binoculars* (Highlands: Jonathan Williams, 1956) was to have been distributed in Canada by the Ryerson Press. Ryerson, however, in effect censored the book by refusing to send out review copies or to supply bookstores. (See Lotta Dempsey, "Poet Attacks Publisher's Attitude," *The Globe and Mail*, 14 Jan. 1957, p. 17). The second, enlarged edition of 1957 was distributed by Contact Press. William Carlos Williams' views on Layton, referred to in letter #51, can be found in his introduction to this book, "A Note on Layton," pp. [9-10]. For further references concerning the "quarrel," see note 3 to letter #46.

2 Smith's *The Oxford Book of Canadian Verse in English and French* (Toronto: Oxford Univ. Press, 1960) was not published until 1960. The 3rd

Elephants and
    Offensives
Down out of impossibilities
    Snows and
    Glaciers
With indignant pachyderm prints in them.
Hannibal succumbed to his victories.
I would be defeated.
Thinking it more just
That you should astound me with amnesia
Without the elephants.

[All the best,
Ralph]

46

62 Delaware Avenue,
Toronto, May 18th, 1957.

Dear Ralph,

I'm sorry not to have replied sooner to your letter of April 22 but some points you brought up required a little thinking about, for example, what *do* the first three lines in Smith's "The Plot Against Proteus" mean; and over and above all that there arrived an extraordinary flood of English literary magazines from Peter Russell far exceeding (in cost) the moderate sum I had sent him to cover my possible book purchases. I had asked him to do what he could, and he did. I now have copies (sometimes up to 8 or 10 each) of *Mandrake, Twentieth Century, London Magazine, Encounter, Lines Review, Zero* (Paris), *Departure, Listen, Quixote, Stand, Poetry and Poverty, Nimbus, Colonnade, Platform*, and *Verse* (No. 1); and I have been busy mulling over these and sorting them out.

Regarding "Proteus":[1] A piece by Smith is likely to be a tour de force, a deliberate 'exercise', display of technique, making use of elements drawn from some one else. Here he draws on Joyce, *Finnegan's Wake*, Anna Livia Plurabelle, in particular, I should say. The changing of word-shapes or

edition of *The Book of Canadian Poetry* was published in 1957.

3 For A.J.M. Smith's "The Plot Against Proteus," see note 1 to letter #46.

1 See A.J.M. Smith, "The Plot Against Proteus," in *The Classic Shade: Selected Poems*, introd. M.L. Rosenthal (Toronto: McClelland

and Stewart, 1978), p. 25. The
last lines read: "...This
cracked walrus skin that
stinks / Of the rank sweat of
a mermaid's thighs / Cast off
and nab him; when you have
him, call."

meanings is tied up by him, very neatly, with Proteus' changes. 'Cornets' is
implied, becoming 'coronets'. The 'dangling from debilitated heads' implies
dethronement, for example, that of Proteus, by capture. My gloss, for whatever it is worth, would run something like this. — This is a theme for muted
music, that is, a *secret* theme. It is about the dethroning, by stealth, of the
elusive: 'heads' meaning 'sources'; the changeable, malleable, if you like, water
imagery coming in; 'kings' to point towards Proteus, named later; it is also a
musical theme (cornets, implied) and this music may be the music of verse,
by one interpretation. That is, it is possible to look on this piece as referring
to, exemplifying, the ability of technical skill to fix the elusive poetic; not
excluding other interpretations, also possible. But of course, when one gets
into this question one may really be indulging in mere fancies, though I suppose that anything the poem suggests to anybody can be taken as 'belonging'
to it. I know Smith thinks very highly of this piece. He remarked to me once
that we had each written one 'perfect piece'. His was this sonnet. I remember
when, long ago, at Hart House (University) he showed me a number of his
poems, I picked on this one, especially the last line.

When I was thinking about "Proteus", the following developed, not a parody, or commentary. So far as I know it means nothing at all except a sort of
punning.

Dicit Proteus Captivus

You took me for a parallellogram
Where two sides never meet. Enough of that!
What's right's not left; what's bulgy can't be flat.
Secure within my watery-weedy calm
For triangles I didn't care a damn, —
Euclidean pinpricks, buzzings of a gnat —
And toyed with mermaids giving tit for tat,
When comes this trickerish interloper. Wham!
No time to shift, I gave one dismal shout.
Futile disguisements vanished into air.
Pinkerton! Pinkerton! Have you caught me out?
A circle? No! We'll leave that to the girls,
Wavy and curvish-like, all whirls and curls.
I claim correction, sir. — I am a 'square'.

Here's another little effort, which I don't 'understand' either; perhaps a
comment on the 'new movement' in England, perhaps a self-parody.

If he hadn't come in out of the rain
I wouldn't have known how wet
he was. Cows, bulldogs,
sheep and nanny-goats are like

That; they get wet
when they stand out
in the rain; elephants too
are the same, they say.

He made a puddle on the floor
(not his fault) and after
another look in the glass
went to bed

Where he ought to be, snugly,
yet — at least I hope so.
Meanwhile his clothes are drying
on the stove. Goodbye for now.

In "Edelweiss" (to make a few comments which you know by this time
are likely to come) it struck me that it might be possible to make the first
two lines more immediately and unmistakably clear. It *might* be considered
that 'move you to love by verse' means 'move you to (express) love by verse'
though of course that's not the meaning — but it is a *remote* possibility
which might be eliminated, perhaps, by putting it 'move you, by verse, to
love'? The repetition of 'movement', or almost repetition, from 'moved' is
always, *in itself*, I think, slightly weakening, but need not be so, in fact the
contrary, under special circumstances (plenty in Milton). The question is —
which is the case here? The moving is of mountainous difficulty, but is the
difficulty attached to the actual movement... no, I'll leave this, I thought for a
moment 'effort' might be feasible, but 'movement' has a wider
connotation — the military movement etc. It occurred to me that the words
'This is' are not strictly necessary? But the line *ought* to have three stresses,
followed by the two of 'diminishing me', so this seems OK. At the end it
seemed to me insufficiently positive in this way, that 'Thinking it more just/
that you should astound me with amnesia', so far, is saying, in a way,

something not intended, emphasizing the justness of being astounded, as such. I'll try to make this clearer by putting it.

> Thinking
> That you should astound me with amnesia
> More just
> Without the elephants.

though this has four lines now instead of the three which, *in itself*, is probably a demerit. I think this is a good little piece with a good idea and probably my emendations are not to the point really, arising from a different, not more valid, feeling for style.

It's going to make this letter a long one if I go into the Dudek-Layton-critics business but I intended to. There *has* been an interchange in the *Forum* in the last few months. I don't know that the *Forum* has 'a lot of good poetry' in it, though they had a large group by Jay Macpherson a few months ago[2] but quite often something of interest — reviews or correspondence — turns up. This dispute ran for a time in the *Queen's Quarterly* I think, till the editor disbarred it. The trouble seems to have been that while Art Smith finally came around to admitting Layton into the canon, with guarded approval, this approval wasn't enthusiastic enough, and Dudek jumped in reproving Smith, and other critics, incidentally. The dispute continued in the *Forum* and I have most of the recent copies, though not all.

In October — A long letter by Layton castigating A.G. Christopher 'of Ile Bigras' for, apparently, writing to the *Forum* re 'coprological verse' (Layton's). In this letter occur, for example: (I mean in Layton's letter) "Those white-livered recreants, Frye, Wilson, Smith, and MacLure", "That old bell-weather, A.J.M. Smith", "the critics and reviewers in this country have been of no help to poets battling this pervasive and odious prudery" etc. It's really a vigorous letter and winds up with a defense of Dudek and Dudek's *Europe*. In January, a very mean review by Kildare R.E. Dobbs of Dudek's *The Transparent Sea*; also a letter from Smith with a very Popish little piece about Layton (and Dudek). He calls *Europe* 'Dudek's ponderous and pompous piece of stale Pound cake.' In February, a short reply from A.W. Purdy to Dobbs' review, with a little piece of verse by Dudek, not bad, 'To Kildare Dobbs'. Purdy's letter, unfortunately, was rather clumsy, and really unfavorable to Dudek while trying to help him! (Dobbs' review annoyed me very much, and after Purdy's letter I wrote a piece I sent to Dudek in one of my letters. I have enclosed it along with another sent to Dudek). In March, there was a little piece of verse 'To Louis Dudek' by Dobbs. In May, Smith, who is

2 Jay Macpherson, "Plowman in Darkness," *The Canadian Forum*, March 1956, pp. 282-83.

really annoyed, apparently, had another Popish piece, longer, which, while I don't exactly approve of such open apeing of Pope, I had better copy out to show you, clearly, the present situation.[3]

On Reading Certain Poems and Epistles of Irving Layton and Louis Dudek   (by A.J.M. Smith)

Hail Coprophilia, muse of Layton, hail!
Doxy of Dudek, skoal! who drop'st in pail
Thick steaming words and brownish lumps of rhyme —
Manure essential in this barren clime,
Where Saxon critics without guts or gall
Praise these thy sons but little, if at all.
Yet these are they who vindicate thy cause,
Who preach thy gospel and affirm thy laws.
Blest pair of poets, put on earth by thee
To sweat and strain and groan to set us free
From Anglo-philistine hypocrisy.
What shovelsful of praise we ought to pay
These swart forerunners of an Augean day
Let us with candour, clangour, and no taste,
Make haste to proffer, O make haste, make haste!
Layton shall how to flatter Layton teach,
And modest Dudek Dudek's glories preach;
LAYTON shall tingle in Canadian air,
And echo answer DUDEK everywhere.
In ev'ry quarterly and magazine
Their linked names in squibs and puffs be seen;
Letters to editors be filled with them,
And gratitude replace each critic's phlegm:
Repentent Wilson, Dobbs, MacLure, and Frye
Shall who can praise them loudest longest, try.

As you will perceive, things seem headed for a free-for-all. If this is the 'ferment in Canada', it exists undoubtedly, of literary value or not. As for people's reading Canadian poetry, of course not, only those who are interested. Layton has sold a lot of his volume in the States, a second edition coming out, and it will be obtainable here from Contact Press (Souster) after Ryerson backed out. Layton *has* brought this matter up in letters to the papers, in Montreal at least — or *someone's* letters or comments did appear —

3 Layton's letter is in *The Canadian Forum*, Oct. 1956, pp. 160-62; Kildare Dobbs's review of Dudek's *The Transparent Sea* is in the issue of Jan. 1957, p. 238, and Smith's letter is in the same issue, p. 237; Purdy's letter is in the issue of Feb. 1957, p. 254, and Dudek's poem "To Kildare Dobbs" is on the same page; Dobbs's poem "To Louis Dudek" is in the March 1957 issue on p. 277; A.J.M. Smith's "On Reading Certain Poems and Epistles of Irving Layton and Louis Dudek" is in *The Canadian Forum*, May 1957, pp. 41-42. The dispute began in *Queen's Quarterly* (see note 3 to letter #44), and at the end of the article by Dudek there is an editor's note that reads in part: "The back-and-forth play of attack, defense, counter-attack and counter-defense is seldom edifying. We believe that this clash of opinion between Smith and Dudek is provocative but that the 'lines of battle' are now clearly enough drawn."

4 For Layton's *Improved Binoculars*, see note 1 to letter #45.

5 Jay Macpherson, "The Fisherman: A Book of Riddles," *The Tamarack Review*, No. 1 (Autumn 1956), pp. 23-29.

but hasn't emphasized it especially, pointing out that Ryerson's offered to give him the 200 copies they had taken.[4]

Tamarack Review. — I'm not greatly taken with it. They had that group by Jay Macpherson, of course.[5] The same Dobbs is an editor, I see, and I certainly felt annoyed by his Dudek review! I prefer *Combustion*.

Another recent 'variation' (nearly all were written in 1948):

Stephen Spender

The waves, at times, threw up a little mist,
Rainbowish colors, — some might call them tosh, —
Vague as the feelings of his personal list —
The whole effect was rather wishy-wash.

Ray Souster thought them 'good fun'.

I hope you are well, and not being too much diverted from poetry.

Yours sincerely,
Eustace Ross

_____

Yes, 'geophysicist etc.' is correct.

[The following two poems were enclosed with this letter]

To Praise or Not to Praise
(Referring to the difficulty and danger associated with making any comment on Canadian poetry, and in particular the poems of Irving Layton)

'Canadian poetry
no matter what, the fate of'
        Charles Olson?

To praise, and not to praise enough
Is fatal. One will suffer
Some slings and arrows (see Art Smith).
Would *not* to praise be tougher?

Encomiums unqualified
By any reservation? —
I feel even here a trap might spring
And drop one to perdition.

For one must tread a wary path
Through willow, oak and hazel
Where birds may sing, but shots will ring —
Pop goes the weasel!

This path's beset by spring-traps, gins,
And ambushes to worry us.
Look neither to the right nor left?
But even that's most hazardous.

"I'd rather live in Oregon"
And eat prairie-dog meat in obscurity
Than, from Toronto,
Have to make any comment on current Canadian poetry.

For instance, it's highly dangerous
To say anything unflattering about E.J. Pratt,
And one may expect a distinct lack of ceremony
In the appropriate tit for tat.

When, for example, some years ago Pratt
Was feeling annoyed by the pretentions of Wilson Macdonald,
He said — What do you suppose? —
"I'd like to punch Wilson Macdonald on the nose."

And even in the very different and much more interesting case
Of Irving Layton
Prudence suggests I should approach the matter of commenting with
Some hesitation.

I see many excellent poems in his collection
Especially, as always, De Bullion Street;
Also, e.g., Love's Diffidence, an astonishing piece,
(The former's probably my favorite);

First Snow; Lake Achigan; "I shall wander all night and not see";
Sacrament By The Water
(Or most of it): Saratoga Beach, ditto; Nausicaa;
The poet's song for his daughter......

But I notice one thing about all these pieces, or nearly all, —
They rhyme;
That is to say, for the most part,
Though not all the time;

And so I conclude that, as far as I am concerned, though I say this
With a certain amount of alarm,
In some of the other poems a little more strictness in the matter of
                                              rhythm (or even rhyme) etc.
Wouldn't do any harm,

Since I think (again one's own opinion) it is from the fusion of 'form' and
                                 'content' (really, of course, not separable)
Or whatever you like to call
The process that, in general, there arises
'Poetry', if at all.

And is it permitted to say (here I reach for my nose-guard)
With still greater hesitation
That in some of the pieces there is a tendency to depend a little too much
                                 on arbitrary, i.e. unsupported, fancies
And rhetorical ornamentation?

Enough's enough!
I would not make
Things too tough
For me, by mistake.

Perhaps it's better to be mum
And simply wait and wait,
Say not a word till kingdom come?
No! Wolves are howling at the gate!

And, taking all in all, I think
Though I've been poised upon the brink
Of a profound abyss
This venturing on some remarks,
Like tid-bits thrown to the sharks,
May show where safety is.
With luck one then may get away

And live to swim another day.
But have I said the exact right thing?
No use at all in worrying!
Silence would be the worst of all
In this important matter.
Unprotected in a squall
Where each word flies like a cannon-ball
And dreadful keen claws tear and maul
The neutral suffers most of all
However trite his part, and small.
Standing with back against the wall
He'll feel — a prospect to appall! —
A flood of bricks that batter —
On him a tower of Babylon fall
With an astounding clatter.

Letter That Might Not Be Sent to an Editor
(concurring in a reader's demand that acerbity in periodical criticism be
suppressed)

When critics' black-marked space is filled
With personalities,
Making the books and authors seem
Tainted by some disease,
Time to put down your foot, insist
They utter nothing mean.
Let's keep these columns clean, dear sir,
Let's keep our columns clean!

Chorus:
Let's keep these columns clean, dear sir,
Let's keep our columns clean!

If critics loathe the stuff they read
Let them endeavor to
Conceal the tenor of their thought
And expurgate their view,
Even if they rank the book
As verging on the obscene.
Let's keep these columns clean, dear sir,
Let's keep our columns clean!

Humor, not venom, is the rule
That should be followed tight,
Though it may make our budding school
Toothless, smooth and trite.
A doctor must not utter oaths
Even before gangrene.
Let's keep these columns clean, dear sir,
Let's keep our columns clean!

Let critics grow in mellowness,
Say "most encouraging,"
"This is the echt-canadian,"
"Really, most promising!" —
No hint of arrière pensée
Tucked away in between.
Let's keep these columns clean, dear sir,
Let's keep our columns clean!

"We'll follow always on his trail,
His headlong, high career.
We do not wish to damp his wing
So let's give one big cheer!
"Surely this derives from some
Pure literary gene."
Let's keep these columns clean, dear sir,
Let's keep our columns clean!⁶

Rough critics should be seen, not heard,
As children — so it's said —
Must either shut up, and behave,
Or else be sent to bed; —
With, for the critic's midnight snack,
A pound of paris green.
Let's keep these columns clean, dear sir,
Let's keep our columns clean!

It's safer for the critic too
To muzzle him in time
Or else he may expose to view
A mind of malice, slime;

6 In the original letter, Ross
has scored through this verse
and written "Omit" in the
margin.

A buzzard staggering to the ground
Bent on some foul repine.
Let's keep these columns clean, dear sir,
Let's keep our columns clean!

For if you muffle So and So
And stifle his heart throbs
How in creation can we know
That he's the Prince of Slobs?
He'll not betray himself if kept
From getting too darn keen.
Let's keep these columns clean, dear sir,
Let's keep our columns clean!

What if the critics be so wrong?
They'll up and at it still.
They cannot hear a new song,
Try as they doubtless will.
But don't permit them to be frank!
Don't let black thoughts be seen!
Let's keep these columns clean, dear sir,
Let's keep our columns clean.

So let his rancor be suppressed
Firmly, for his own sake —
The sophomoric witless ass
May make some grave mistake. —
And save the critics from themselves
By bottling up their spleen.
Let's keep these columns clean, dear sir,
Let's keep our columns clean!

We do not want too honest talk,
The statement that is clear,
And we reject with emphasis
Anything too sincere;
For what this country chiefly needs
Is cultural hygiene.
Let's keep these columns clean, dear sir,
Let's keep our columns clean!

Chorus:
Let's keep these columns clean, dear sir,
Let's keep our columns clean!

47

2 West 67th Street
New York 23, N.Y.
June 17, 1957

Dear Eustace,

I don't suppose it matters — what 'meaning' the Proteus sonnet carries. I
hadn't thought of the possible theme being "the elusive poetic". May be. All I
know is that Menelaus covered with a stinking seal-skin lay amongst the
flock of Proteus' seals to capture Proteus the prophetic sea-god, and made
him tell him how he could secure a southerly breeze so that he could get
home with Helen from Egypt to Sparta again. I know Art thinks highly of
this sonnet (and his "The Archer"). You do not say what poem of yours he
named as a "perfect piece"? I would name "The Walk".
    Your "Dicit Proteus Captivus" amused me immensely.
    I wrote a piece called "The Election":

I saw the years
And the years' fall
Carthage's salt
And the villa that
Hadrian built
And the bridge
Over Provence
For water
And the trestle
In the valley of
The Massawippi
That linked
Oceans
That made a nation
And I thought
Of the robin's egg

Blue
And the diamond in the earth
And of Athens
And how you lay
To time to time
Not naked
But in the provenance
Of empires and Sardanapalus
Nude.[1]

1 "The Election" was collected in *Rivers Among Rocks*, poem #17.

Don't ask me how the Eastern Township trestle got mixed up in the empires.

I enjoyed your account of the Layton-Dudek-Smith affair hugely. Art Smith has really praised Layton — and has five pieces of Layton in his *Oxford Bk of Cdn Verse*. Smith is really a wit — and handles his barbs superbly. The coprology in Layton is really irrelevant. What he is is really immensely tender. As for Mr. Kildare Dobbs — he recently returned five or six of my poems sent up for *Tamarack Review*. I, of course think less than nothing of him. But ... apart from all this ... *Tamarack Review* is a pretty limp effort. It's smart and current-newsy and the prose is execrable.

The Anthology is done — except I must revise the Introduction. In it I try to deal with what distinguishes Cdn poetry as Cdn. I deal with the thrust of personality of E.J. Pratt after the Pickthall-twilight, and then say that "A modern awareness, with its concommitant, experimentation with technique, a reduction of Canada, of the quality of Canada, were entering into Canadian verse. W.W.E. Ross' "northern" poems were written almost entirely in one night in April 1928, in northern Ontario. They captured precisely, with wonder and freshness, a distinct Canada. The rural parallel, is Raymond Knister."

All right?

The last of the copyright permissions is in — except for P. Page's — she is very upstage — perhaps as ambassadress to Brazil — certainly not as a poet — and the book is going to cost a fortune!

All the best.

Yours,
Ralph

48

62 Delaware Ave,
Toronto, June 19/57

Dear Ralph,

Thank you for your letter. This is a hasty note to point out a slight correction in your reference to me in the Introduction to your anthology. It wasn't "*in* Northern Ontario," but rather "remembering" N.O. since the pieces were written in Toronto after a lively evening's discussion of Canadian nationalism. My survey trips were in 1912 and 1913. I thought it an interesting coincidence that the first began, by canoe, at the same point on the C.P.R. (Kapuskasing) where Tom Thomson had left the railway the year before on his first serious sketching trip (by canoe). In 1913 we were north of Lake Superior (near the group of seven's 'Algoma country', and further west).

I've been completely detached from poetry this last month having switched to other 'projects' or 'studies'. I concentrate on one at a time. Anne Wilkinson calls herself the 'sports editor' of *Tamarack Review* and claims the board of editors won't let her express certain ideas she has. So I doubt her responsibility for the 'execrable prose'. I don't know *who* has written the editorials, for example — perhaps Kildare Dobbs? I didn't send them anything myself, so didn't have the pleasure of a rejection. The magazine does seem *tame* somehow. (I *won't* make a pun about the name here).

I'll leave concentrating on your piece "The Election" until I have returned to the 'vibration' of poetry, (as they say in spiritualistic circles).

I must get this in the mail.

Yours sincerely,
Eustace Ross

49

2 West 67th Street
New York 23, N.Y.
June 21, 1957

Dear Eustace,

Many thanks for sending me down so promptly the correction of my remark
in the Introduction to the anthology. I've set things straight.

The Anthology goes off next week to England for setting. I am not sorry
to see the last of it — though I of course liked doing it.

All the best,

Sincerely
Ralph

50

Apt 2D
515 West 168th
New York 32, N.Y.
February 24, 1959

Dear Eustace,

I enclose my cheque for $25 in payment of the poems of yours reprinted in
The Penguin Book of Canadian Verse — with many thanks for your
cooperation — I was very glad to have the poems.

I haven't had many reactions to the book yet — but on the whole I think
the critics think it is a good book. Only one review out of Toronto — except
the last issue of *Tamarack* — and a few others in Canada.[1] So I don't suppose
people know about it — but I am hoping it goes well. I had hopes this one
would go better than the last one (being certainly better) — but I don't know.

Anything new of yours appearing? I've been trying to gather together
some poems that wouldn't represent me too badly and finally, yesterday, got
the typescript off to McClelland & Stewart, who are bringing the book out in

1 *The Penguin Book of Canadian Verse* was reviewed in
The Tamarack Review, No.
10 (Winter 1959), pp. 101-02.

their Indian File Series this fall. I've called it *Rivers Among Rocks* — a kind of pessimistic-optimistic title, I suppose, but one I took from *Job*.[2]

All the best wishes,

As ever,
Ralph

51

Lake Scugog,
August 19-1959.

Dear Ralph,

I should have thanked you long ago for the cheque but for several months I wrote, and read, practically nothing. Here, at the lake, I've been catching up on both. We're here for three weeks and my address remains, of course, 62 Delaware.

Glad to learn a book of your poems will be coming out this fall. It wasn't till after considerable delay that I got hold of a copy of the Penguin anthology. I haven't been going down town because of lack of time and the parking difficulties. Mary tried Eaton's unsuccessfully, finally secured a copy at Simpson's. I've been going over it carefully, and find it somewhat more diffuse than the first one, more like Smith's — though the introduction is certainly breezier than his. It's so much bigger, and with all that Roberts, Carman etc. it seems more literary-historical, less "modern". The late nineteenth century English (and American) poetic annals (periodicals, etc.) must have been filled with similar echoes of Keats, Shelley and others and their recent anthologists have tended to drop most of it, even when (in the U.S.) the anthology claims to be 'from the beginning'. Was it the big Stedman (?) collection that still carried a full load of it?[1] Anyway, for me, reading large gobs of Roberts and the others is like trying to swallow a mass of feathers from a slit pillow. I won't enlarge on this. Isn't Lampman's "Life and Nature" (Oh, Life! Oh, Life!) simply one of the silliest pieces ever written, if you examine it closely — and all because he either didn't like organ music or happened to run into some bad organists ('moaning shrill')? And "The Piper of Arll" has always been one of my pet aversions. (I could go on at great length but

2 *Rivers Among Rocks* was not published until 1960, and then not as part of the "Indian File" series, but as the first of a group of books beautifully designed by Frank Newfeld. As Gustafson refers to the slow progress of this book in several of the following letters, it may be worth giving the full story here. The collection was submitted to McClelland and Stewart in May 1958, and formally accepted on October 14. After some revisions were made, the final typescript reached the publisher in February 1959. In the fall of that year, McClelland and Stewart decided to discontinue the "Indian File" series and to issue *Rivers Among Rocks* instead as a deluxe collector's book. The book did not go to the printer until the spring of 1960, and first proofs were sent to Gustafson on April 27. Manufacturing proceeded very slowly, and copies were not in Gustafson's hands until late December 1960, though the official date of publication was 16 January 1961. (I am grateful to McClelland and Stewart for permission to read the files on this book in the McClelland and Stewart papers at McMaster University Library.)

1 Edmund Clarence Stedman, ed., *An American Anthology, 1787-1900: Selections Illustrating the Editor's Critical Review of American Poetry in the Nineteenth Century* (Cambridge: Riverside, 1900).

won't.) Anyway, I don't see how those writers can have the faintest stimulating effect on young writers nowadays, who very properly look elsewhere, and, if they want romanticism, take it straight, from the best sources. *The Revolt of Islam* was a great big unsuccessful attempt by Shelley to use the Spenserian stanza, and Sangster's Spenserians are simply an echo of bad Shelley. When I was young, of all that 19th century 'serious' Canadian poetry Heavysege's sonnets seemed to have a curious, strange quality, and I could take a *little* Crawford, but that is almost all, and I still feel about the same.

Of course I appreciate the difficulty a Canadian anthologist is up against. The horrid fact is that Canada, differing from the U.S., England and France, didn't have *any* first rate poets in the 19th century (and I'm doubtful about the 20th century too, so far!). The situation must be the same in Australia, New Zealand and South Africa. There must be 'pet' earlier poets who are claimed to be essentially 'Australian', etc., and are carefully preserved, rather to the bewilderment of the outside world. Here, since a country, to be a 'nation' *must* have a great poet, or great poets, some of the most (apparently) modern minded have fallen back on Pratt. (See the late John Sutherland for example.)[2] This too is rather confusing to the Americans and British. Some Americans, Robert Creeley, I think, and W.C. Williams look on Layton as the first Canadian 'great' (possibly) poet.[3] And so the process continues. Similarly, in Germany, Goethe was hoisted into that position, since Germany had to have a great poet, but with considerable excuse. Personally I'd put Holderlin in that position, although at the time Goethe and Schiller finally came to refusing to answer his letters. (Pratt on Layton — "I *hate* Layton." It used to be "I'd like to punch Wilson Macdonald on the nose.") The thing to do, apparently, is to be really vociferous about one's talent — though there may be, finally, a big flop, as in the case of Amy Lowell.

I'm a little curious as to the writer of the lines (p. 25) on 'the specifics of contemporary Canadian poetry.'[4] I assume it is yourself, but you didn't make that clear in your radio talk on the subject. Marianne Moore once remarked in a letter to me that she thought Birney the most 'Canadian' poet, which was a little confusing to me since she had previously indicated that the only piece by him she really liked was "Slug in Woods". She couldn't 'see' Pratt as was apparent from her reply when John Sutherland sent her a copy of the *Northern Review* number in which he proclaimed Pratt a 'great' poet.

I'll certainly be interested in learning how this collection sells, and in any critical comments, especially from the U.S. and England.

You asked if anything new of mine is appearing. I've sent nothing out for over a year, but notice that Dudek is still printing the odd little piece from

2 There was a Pratt issue of the *Northern Review*, 5, No. 3 and No. 4 (Feb.-March and April-May 1952). Sutherland's "E.J. Pratt: A Major Contemporary Poet" is on pp. 36-64. See also note 2 to letter #36.

3 In a review published in the first issue of the *Black Mountain Review*, Creeley wrote that "Layton may well be, for the historian of literature at any rate, the first great Canadian poet ...." See "Canadian Poetry 1954," reprinted in *A Quick Graph: Collected Notes and Essays*, ed. Donald Allen (San Francisco: Four Seasons Foundation, 1970), p. 232. For William Carlos Williams' view of Layton, see note 1 to letter #45.

4 On p. 24 of *The Penguin Book of Canadian Verse*, Gustafson asks: 'What is Cana-

dian? The specifics of contemporary Canadian poetry are these," following which is a list of themes and attributes.

5 W. W. E. Ross, "Anti-archetypal," *Delta*, No. 3 (April 1958), p. 30; "In Defence of Critics" and "Think of That," *Delta*, No. 7 (April 1959), p. 5; and "Morning," *Delta*, No. 8 (July 1959), p. 18.

among a group sent to him over a year ago.[5]

With best wishes for the success of your forthcoming book,

Yours sincerely,
Eustace Ross

_____

52
_____

c/o A. J. M. Smith
640 Bailey Street
East Lansing, Mich.
Sept. 28/59

Dear Eustace,

I'm still on a trans-Canada journey that has taken the past three months, but want to drop a note in reply to yours of August 19th.[1] Sorry that it should have been so long unanswered. I am back eastward after a long time in the Rockies, Yukon and the Pacific coast; eventually for a reading of poems at the Isaacs Gallery in Toronto on Oct [3]rd;[2] thence, home to N.Y. to collect gathered thoughts. I did though manage to get a book of poems written in the Rockies (as soon as the mist closed in and I couldn't find escape in the trails).[3] Trust the *Penguin Book of Cdn Verse* didn't choke you with too many 19th century feathers. I still think some good poems were written then by Canadians. What would one do on the principle that poets weakly hark back to others? Read only Shakespeare? Anyway, if one has to survey Canadian verse, one has to survey Canadian verse. And I made the book almost two/thirds contemporary — and so hoped for the best. Yes, the "specifics" were my own. I didn't fool around with them. An amusing list, n'est ce pas? The Australians find us "vital"; the British find us (when they do at all) "aggressive". All the best. It was good to hear from you. Please repeat, if you will...

Ever,
Ralph

_____

1 Gustafson had a Canada Council Senior Fellowship during 1959-60. He and his wife Betty spent several months (beginning in July 1959) travelling across Canada.

2 This reading was part of the Contact Poetry Readings series.

3 Ralph Gustafson, *Rocky Mountain Poems* (Vancouver: Klanak, 1960).

53

515 West 168th Street
New York 32, N.Y.
August 13, 1960

Dear Eustace,

The enclosed letter reached me here in PEI where my wife and I are having a holiday.[1] As it is now pretty old I did not want your poem to miss being in the anthology. I have also written to Miss Harris giving her your address and saying that you own the copyright.[2]

I was up in Kingston in June and saw various poets; all seems to be in lively ferment. Earle Birney has his collected poems coming out (his Far Eastern poems are exciting); Art Smith has been asked for a volume from Knopf; I haven't seen Margaret Avison's book yet but have ordered it. Louis Dudek goes off on a C[anada] C[ouncil grant] to Europe, I believe. Irving [Layton] blew into a session, exploded in fine fettle, read some poems next day, and blew out.[3]

Two years now since McClelland & Stewart accepted my ms of poems. Still no book! However, I have corrected the gallies and the page-proofs are supposed to reach me here for final correction; and they say September is the publication month. I'll believe it when I see it. Anyway, a handsome book in format when it does appear. The *Rocky Mountain Poems* come out this October from Klanak Press.

Hope you thrive personally and poetically?

All best wishes,
Ralph

1 The Gustafsons were vacationing at Cavendish, Prince Edward Island.

2 Ross has noted on this letter that the request was from McClelland and Stewart.

3 The occasion for this meeting was the conference of the Humanities Association held at Queen's University. Gustafson gave a poetry reading there on June 16.

54

515 West 168th Street
New York 32, N.Y.
August 31, 1960

Dear Eustace,

1 As noted by Ross, this request was from the publisher Schofield & Sims, Ltd.

Another request for a poem of yours in the Penguin anthology.[1] I send the enclosed along as you will want to handle this direct.

    All best wishes,

Ralph

55

62 Delaware Ave,
Toronto, Ont, Oct. 24/60.

Dear Ralph, —

Too belatedly I must thank you for forwarding to me two requests for "The Diver" — one from Miss Harris, at Winnipeg; and the other from England (Schofield and Son). I acceded to both, and wrote them. You must be sick and tired of sending me requests of this sort — and they're all for the same piece, and all for school-books. However, that is how things are! I guess my style is *simple*, to say the least!

    I was shocked to see your piece "Obiit" in *Delta* #12, p. 25.[1] Surely there's something wrong somewhere. As I remember the 1st edition sold more profusely? Is everybody deadened by T.V. etc?

    Saw Art. Smith at a cocktail party at *Amen House* (Oxford) re the anthology (the drinks were stronger than one should have expected at *Amen* etc), but he didn't say anything about his Knopf volume.[2] However I was speaking to him only for a moment.

    I do hope you get some satisfaction out of McClelland and Stewart re your own book, and hope to see the *Rocky Mt. Poems* somewhere in these parts.

1 Ralph Gustafson, "Obiit," *Delta*, No. 12 (Sept. 1960), p. 25. Gustafson complained bitterly in this brief piece about the Canadian sales of the *Penguin Book of Canadian Verse*.

2 No book by A.J.M. Smith was published by Knopf.

First (2 years ago) the imminence and then (this summer) the actuality of retirement from my Dominion Government post as scientific officer have been harder to "take" than I should ever have imagined. However, I think all is well, and hope *you* are as you say "thriving personally and poetically." The very best. —

Yours sincerely,
Eustace Ross

56

515 West 168th Street
New York 32, N.Y.
November 22, 1960

Dear Eustace,

It was good to have your letter — and less than no trouble to me is it, to send along those requests for your poems deriving out of the Penguin. It's satisfying to know how deep "The Diver" dives. I thought the group Art Smith chose of yours for his new Anthology, excellent. It would be a good and satisfying thing if a collected book of your poems was done. Do you not think of this?

McClelland & Stewart still dawdle over my book *Rivers Among Rocks*. It is going on three years now since the contract was signed. Jack McC[lelland] blames the printer & ultimately the designer for the delay. I write constant letters to prod *him*. He now tells me that December 8th is the publication day. I sincerely trust so. *Rocky Mt Poems* is out. The latest news of the Penguin collection is nil — as far as I know. They bungled the reviewing job and they bungled the distribution. But I hope it is a long-range book. I thought at the inexpensive price Canada might have wanted it.

I see Margaret Avison reads here at the YMHA next February. How have the readings in Toronto gone?

It would be good to see you. We dont get to Toronto often — but perhaps the new book might bring us up, in some capacity. I have been doing mostly music reviews for the CBC. Nine hours of programs on "Masters of the

1 Pianist Sviatoslav Richter.

Keyboard" — and the last stint, a review of Richter[1] N.Y. recitals for CBC "Music Diary".

All warmest best wishes,

Sincerely
Ralph

_____

57
_____

515 West 168th Street
New York 32, N.Y.
December 17, 1960

Dear Eustace,

1 A request from *World Digest*, as noted by Ross on this letter.

This enclosed came this morning.[1] It's wonderful — the force of your poems. Best wishes.

Happy New Year!

Sincerely,
Ralph

_____

I've written the editor saying the copyright is yours.

58
_____

62 Delaware Ave.,
Toronto, Dec. 27/60.

Dear Ralph,

1 I have not been able to discover that "The Diver" was in fact ever reprinted in *World Digest*.

Thank you again for forwarding to me a request for reprinting pieces of mine (*World Digest*).[1] Really you *must* be bored with this sort of thing. And thank you also for your remark about the "force of your poems". This is something hard for me to understand. Was my best "work" really nearly my earliest? Seems so! (Thanks also for telling the *W. D.* editor the copyright is mine. I'm hazy on this subject of copyright!). Of course I'm giving permission though I don't know what *World Digest* is, — probably a quarterly?

Re your letter of Nov. 20 which I find I haven't replied to, — yes, of course, I've thought of a "book" — but it seems as though one had to put up one's own money and take a chance on sales (not that I've "submitted" anything to a publisher). But to drop this subject let me congratulate you on your *increase* in poetic activity recently. And evidently I'm not well briefed on your activities, when you mention doing music reviews, and you seem to be someone of tremendous activity!

Wish I could say the same for myself. The imminence and actuality (last June) of retirement had a most *dampening* effect. It seemed to effect my keenness about other things, poetry, for example, on which I had counted for future activity. I know not all men are affected this way, and hope it's a passing phase.

With kindest regards

> Yours sincerely
> Eustace Ross

59

P.O. Box 172
North Hatley, Que.
April 3, 1964

Dear Eustace,

Longmans, Green & Co. Ltd (48 Grosvenor St. London W.1.) want to reprint 2 of your poems ("Fish", "The Diver") from the Penguin Anthology. I sent them your address & no doubt you'll be hearing. This is nice. Over the years, I think you win about requests for reprints!

I've joined the English Dept at Bishop's[1] — and "taught" your poetry the other day. The "Northern" group was written before the 'twenties; am I not right?

Are you writing now? I would like to have anything new of yours. I was in the vein before I left New York — but the work-load here soon squelched

1 Gustafson began teaching at Bishop's University in Lennoxville, Quebec in 1963.

2 Ralph Gustafson, "The Horses of Saint Mark's" and "On Seeing in a Gothenburg Art Gallery on a Picasso a Blackeye," *Harper's Bazaar*, June 1963, p. 56; "At the Tomb of Galla Placidia, Empress of the West: Ravenna" and "The Swans at Vadstena," *Harper's Bazaar*, Oct. 1963, p. 232.

that; have had one or two groups of poems in *Harper's Bazaar*,[2] but that is about all.

All best wishes,

Yours,
Ralph

60

62 Delaware Ave.,
Toronto 4, Ont.,
April 30/64

Dear Ralph, —

Thanks indeed for sending my address to Longmans, Green & Co. England. You must be tired of these little chores! But it's *your* fault, after all, for picking out those pieces for your anthology. It's most interesting to learn that you are at Bishop's College (or University). Years ago, at Petawawa, my parents were friends of a Col. Aylmer and his wife there. He had something to do with the military camp and was, it is said, a brother of "Lord Aylmer". Anyway, they came from Lennoxville, and I wonder if the name "Aylmer" means anything there.[1]

The "Northern" group was written in 1928. (As a matter of fact one of them "The Saws were Shrieking" narrowly escaped being destroyed by me during re-examination.)

No, I'm not writing now, not for some time, but have been waiting patiently for a renewal of my "edge" in the matter of poetry.

Some time ago the *New York Times* Daily asked me to submit something (25 lines or under); said they had noticed I had never sent them anything. I didn't feel like doing so just then but tried 3 pieces recently. They took two, printed Feb 27th and April 10th on the Editorial page. I don't think you have seen them — "The Medici Tombs" and "Fall Wheat in Spring".[2]

I was very glad to hear from you, and hope you will pardon my delay in replying — Perhaps it was partly due to my wanting to let you know what

1 Ross is probably referring to Col. Matthew Aylmer (1842-1923) who was born at Melbourne, Quebec (not Lennoxville). After service in the British army, he joined the militia in 1871 and eventually became Adjutant-General of the Militia. He succeeded to a baronetcy on his father's death in 1901.

2 W.W.E. Ross, "The Medici Tombs (Michelangelo)," *The New York Times*, 27 Feb. 1964, p. 30, and "Fall Wheat

Longmans had in mind. Try and guess. Right! "Fish" and "The Diver"! I hope you are in the best of health and enjoying your work.

in Spring," *The New York Times* 16 April 1964, p. 36 (not April 10, as Ross states).

Yours sincerely,
Eustace Ross

61

P.O. Box 172
North Hatley, Que.
May 22, 1964

Dear Eustace,

The name "Aylmer" wakes a far-distant memory — I am sure I knew an Aylmer as a boy in Sherbrooke. Alas, that is far too long ago.

The forwarding chores about your poems in the Anthology are indeed not chores. I suppose over the years, you must have had a half-dozen requests? Gratifying. I gave a lecture on your work this year in my course in Cdn Lit — putting you in one of the thunder bolts that dispersed the left-over purple afterglow of the Romantics. I had some quotations from your poems in the papers of the students. Does one "study" poetry?

Yes, I'd clipped out your poem "The Medici Tombs" from the *N.Y. Times* (but missed the Spring one). Had you been recently to Florence? My wife & I were there two summers ago — and I got the enclosed out of the visit. If at all possible, we hope to get back there next summer.

All good wishes,

Ralph

from *The Year of Voyages*

Michelangelo: The Duomo Workyard

I think old. But two? — years — another
At this Carrara — the first reality, how long

Ago? standing on his platform nude —
Naked — whose smell, now, rather, disgusts me —
Are enough. A third Nativity! making
This grandeur, on this plank at night in sweat wondering:
One more lack of marble between the legs —
The axis cut, the progenitor of holy Jesus
On the floor. They told me. No one can make
The *knot* possible. The terror at night, costs —
Somewhere in the eyes, a rubbing of them —
I beatify my ugliness — rubbing marble
Dust in them. A cost of the future! The magnificence
Takes more than a weariness bargained for.
Well, I've had him, who smells of garlic and sex
Rather too strongly — sometimes. That ton
Is taken on the right foot. I should have cut
Something nobler ... Piccolomini's commission,
Fifteen figures draped stuffed in an altar:
Apollo ballless in the Belvedere.
God's image gets in the way. Granacci
Expostulates: David had no foreskin. He
Smells also. I do. The flint to strike this oil
To fire ...
          So. So stands Jesus. David.
Giombo. Florence. The lip should have more disdain ...

— Ralph Gustafson

I don't know why Browning should have a monopoly!

62

62 Delaware Ave.,
Toronto 4, Ont.,
June 10/64

Dear Ralph, —

Thank you for your letter of May 22 with the poem "Michelangelo: The
Duomo Workyard". I've been very rusty on poetry for some time but this

piece does seem to me a very imaginative depiction of the probable feeling of the aging sculptor. (I didn't quite understand the *knot* and haven't located Granani). It was a little hard to get into but I seem to like the piece better every time I read it.

No, we've never been to Florence. "The Tombs" was written after seeing a photo in a Florence brochure, or in *Time* magazine. I'm enclosing the other piece.

I'm afraid my ignorance, generally, of sculpture and Michelangelo is rather profound!

Pardon the "Spring" copy dirtiness, etc. — one of a number of carbons that have been lying around.

I'm trying to get "going" again in poetry (judgement, creativity etc.) Just now E.E. Cummings — a book about him by someone at Louisiana University[1] — seems stimulating.

With all the best,

Yours sincerely,
Eustace Ross

_____

1 I have not been able to locate any study of Cummings by anyone "at Louisiana University." Possibly Ross was reading Norman Friedman's *E.E. Cummings: The Growth of a Writer* (Carbondale: Southern Illinois Univ. Press, 1964), which had appeared in March of 1964.

Fall Wheat in Spring

How lovely is the green fall wheat!
All winter long, beneath the snow,
It held a promise nascent in
A sleep beneath the whitest sheet!
How beautiful the green of the wheat!

Assurance of the living bread,
Ripeness, and earlier harvest too
If but, propitiously, rain come,
And the summer sun, to bring to a head —
How sweet the promise of the bread!

Golden will be its afterglow,
This jewel changing in its hue.
Emerald, sun will soon unfold,
Produce a gift, unique, to show
A glorious golden afterglow.

Its morning green, its afternoon
Yellowed in maturity —
The close-packed heads will nod in the breeze,
Ripples will follow the wind soon
In its golden opulent afternoon.

Soon, now, this richest green expanse
Will be a sea of rippling blades
in the breeze, in the August afternoon.
Here is the harvest ready to hand
And a thankfulness along the land.

63

62 Delaware Ave.,
Toronto 4, Ont.
June 20/64[1]

Dear Ralph,

In my recent note to you I omitted a comment on typographical errors. In "The Medici Tombs", (*N.Y. Times* 2/27/64), it ought to be "Figure of Night" ... (with a capital N). Again "above the Night", should be followed by a comma, not a period, obviously. Such slips have bothered me much in the past. For example in Smith's latest edition[2] (not in The Oxford Book) in "The Creek" the last line runs "From depths of green unknown" — *not* "dream", which introduces a sort of late romantic vagueness, that I feel should be avoided. This error appeared in a typescript sent me by Smith after his selection of the piece. I pointed out the error as well as some changes I wanted in the "Sonnet" etc. — but apparently (three years later!) the stuff was rushed to the publisher *without* the corrections! Perhaps you've had the same experience. I estimate about 50% of printings have an error or errors somewhere. I've felt at times I'd rather have nothing printed at all than see these annoying mistakes. (I must say that your printings of my pieces are quite clear of any such errors — quite an achievement!)

Regarding "Michelangelo: The Duomo Workshop" — I find it fascinating as I said, but now am beginning to feel my usual dubieties (I mean regarding my interpretation) — Is he really old or just thinking an old man's thoughts?

1 This letter exists only as Ross's draft among his papers at the University of Toronto Library, though Ross has quite clearly marked it "sent." Another draft letter among the Ross papers, dated "early June/64," I have not included here, as it is in note form only and is for the most part illegible.

2 In the 3rd edition of A.J.M. Smith's *The Book of Canadian Poetry* (Toronto: Gage, 1957), Ross's poem "The Creek" concludes with the lines "the stream issuing / from depths of dream unknown."

I wish I had studied his life history, I feel his [impact?] so strongly.

With best regards,

Yours sincerely,
Eustace Ross

64

P.O. Box 172
North Hatley, Que.
July 6, 1964

Dear Eustace,

I have to thank you for two letters. Betty and I have been to New York City for three weeks or I would have responded sooner. Michelangelo was again brought to mind — they have his Pieta in the Vatican Pavilion at the world's fair. One stands on a revolving belt of floor and is slowly drawn across in front of the sculpture. Most effective for avoiding congestion — but not for aesthetic indigestion.

My Michelangelo soliloquy was meant to convey Michelangelo's thoughts as he lay at night in the Duomo workyard where he was working on his "David". The thoughts strike the young sculptor as the thoughts of an old man. I hope this is conveyed clearly? David has taken him three years to carve — he is weary and impatient — as if he were an old man with not much of life left. As for "knot" — I have a pun on the word. He had to beg for a piece of marble that had been abandoned in the cathedral workshop. The marble had a flaw in it (technically called a "knot" in the marble) & it was declared impossible to carve. Michelangelo got around the flaw by carving David's body *turned* in posture. He was told "No one can make the *knot* possible." My pun of course is "No one can make the *not* possible."

I too have been plagued by typographical errors in printed poems. Both my sonnets in the Modern Library *New Anthology of Modern Poetry*[1] have bad errors in them. In "On the Struma Massacre", the line "Studied in ignorance, and knowing Thee" should end with a period; and in "SSR, Lost at Sea", "*These* fantastic in the murk" should be "*There* fantastic etc." In my last book *Rivers Among Rocks*, the poem "A Candle for Pasch" has "Nail and thorn /

1 See letter #39 and note #1 thereto.

And Pale stratagem." for "Nail and thorn / *Are* Pale stratagem." The former of course makes nonsense of the whole stanza. As for the junk they put on the dust-wrapper, I revised their whole galley of it — the revision was completely ignored.

Arthur Smith is aware of the flaw in the printing of your poem "The Creek" in his Anthology. When he inscribed my copy, he corrected in his hand "dream" to "green".

It's like music. Scholars are still correcting the scores of Chopin, Beethoven, etc. I suppose each correction results in flaws in other places!

All best regards,

Sincerely,
Ralph

Index

Bibliography

Avison, Margaret. "Five Poems." *Poetry* [Chicago], 70, No. 6 (Sept. 1947), 318-23.

Benet, William Rose. Rev. of *Brébeuf and His Brethren*, by E.J. Pratt. *Saturday Review of Literature*, 16 Oct. 1943, p. 24.

————. Rev. of *Still Life and Other Verse*, by E.J. Pratt. *Saturday Review of Literature*, 29 April 1944, p. 23.

Birney, Earle. "David." *The Canadian Forum*, Dec. 1941, pp. 274-76.

————. *David and Other Poems*. Toronto: Ryerson, 1942.

————, ed. *Twentieth Century Canadian Poetry: An Anthology With Introduction and Notes*. Toronto: Ryerson, 1953.

Brinnin, John Malcolm. "Views of the Favorite Mythologies." *Poetry* [Chicago], 65, No. 3 (Dec. 1944), 157-60.

Brown. E.K. Rev. of *Anthology of Canadian Poetry (English)*, by Ralph Gustafson. *University of Toronto Quarterly*, 12, No. 3 (April 1943), 311-12.

————. Rev. of *Flight Into Darkness*, by Ralph Gustafson. *University of Toronto Quarterly*, 14, No. 3 (April 1945), 263.

Bulfinch, Thomas. *Mythology: The Age of Fable, The Age of Chivalry, Legends of Charlemagne*. New York: Thomas Y. Crowell Company, 1970.

Callaghan, Morley. *Now That April's Here and Other Stories*. New York: Random House, 1936.

————. *A Native Argosy*. New York: Scribner's, 1929.

Chalmers, J.W., and H.T. Coutts, eds. *Prose and Poetry for Canadians: Enjoyment*. [Toronto]: Dent, 1951.

Crawley, Alan. "Notes on Some Reading." *Contemporary Verse*, 2, No. 5 (Sept. 1942), 15-16.

Creeley, Robert. *A Quick Graph: Collected Notes and Essays*. Ed. Donald Allen. San Francisco: Four Seasons Foundation, 1970.

Creighton, Alan. Rev. of *Flight Into Darkness*, by Ralph Gustafson. *The Canadian Forum*, Dec. 1944, p. 216.

Darling, Michael, ed. "On Poetry and Poets: The Letters of W.W.E. Ross to A.J.M. Smith." *Essays on Canadian Writing*, No. 16 (Fall-Winter 1979-80), pp. 78-125.

Deacon, William Arthur. "Penguin Canadian Anthology Stresses Work of New Poets." *The Globe and Mail*, 6 June 1942, p. 9.

Dempsey, Lotta. "Poet Attacks Publisher's Attitude." *The Globe and Mail*, 14 Jan. 1957, p. 17.

Dobbs, Kildare R. E. Rev. of *The Transparent Sea*, by Louis Dudek. *The Canadian Forum*, Jan. 1957, p. 238.

———. "To Louis Dudek." *The Canadian Forum*, March 1957, p. 277.

Dudek, Louis. "Layton Now and Then: Our Critical Assumptions." *Queen's Quarterly*, 63, No. 2 (Summer 1956), [291]-93.

———. "To Kildare Dobbs." *The Canadian Forum*, Feb. 1957, p. 254.

Gregory, Horace. *Chelsea Rooming House*. New York: Covici, Friede, 1930.

———. "Hellbabies and Others." *Blues: A Magazine of New Rhythms*, 1, No. 5 (1929), 125-28.

———. *Poems 1930-1940*. New York: Harcourt, Brace, 1941.

Gustafson, Ralph. "Anthology and Revaluation." *University of Toronto Quarterly*, 13, No. 2 (Jan. 1944), 229-35.

———, ed. *Anthology of Canadian Poetry (English)*. Harmondsworth: Penguin, 1942.

———. "Apropos of Canadian Poetry." *Tomorrow*, 4, No. 3 (Nov. 1944), 73-74.

———. "At the Tomb of Galla Placidia, Empress of the West: Ravenna." *Harper's Bazaar*, Oct. 1963, p. 232.

———, ed. *Canadian Accent: A Collection of Stories and Poems by Contemporary Writers from Canada*. Harmondsworth: Penguin, 1944.

———. "The Circus." *Tomorrow*, 8, No. 8 (April 1949), 21-25.

———. *Epithalamium in Time of War*. New York: L.F. White, 1941.

———. *Flight Into Darkness*. New York: Pantheon, 1944.

———. "The Horses of Saint Mark's." *Harper's Bazaar*, June 1963, p. 56.

———, ed. *A Little Anthology of Canadian Poets*. Norfolk: New Directions, 1943.

———. *Lyrics Unromantic*. New York: L.F. White, 1942.

———. "Obiit." *Delta*, No. 12 (Sept. 1960), p. 25.

———. "On Seeing in a Gothenburg Art Gallery on a Picasso a Blackeye." *Harper's Bazaar*, June 1963, p. 56.

———. ed. *The Penguin Book of Canadian Verse*. Harmondsworth: Penguin, 1958.

———. *Poetry and Canada*. Ottawa: Canadian Legion Educational Services, 1945.

———. *Rivers Among Rocks*. Toronto: McClelland and Stewart, 1960.

———. *Rocky Mountain Poems*. Vancouver: Klanak, 1960.

———. "The Story of the Penguin." *Canadian Poetry: Studies/Documents/Reviews*, No. 12 (Spring-Summer 1983), pp. 71-76.

————. "The Swans at Vadstena." *Harper's Bazaar*, Oct. 1963, p. 232.

————, ed. *Voices No. 113, Spring 1943.*

"Gustafson's Verse Highly Modernistic." Toronto Daily Star, 30 Dec. 1944, p. 26.

Hambleton, Ronald, ed. *Unit of Five*. Toronto: Ryerson, 1944.

Humphries, Rolfe. "What Price Recognition?". *The New Republic*, 8 May 1944, pp. 634, 636.

Kennedy, Leo. "Raymond Knister." *The Canadian Forum*, Sept. 1932, pp. 459-61.

Klein, A.M. *The Hitleriad*. New York: New Directions, 1944.

————. *Poems*. Philadelphia: Jewish Publication Society, 1944.

Knister, Raymond. *Collected Poems of Raymond Knister*. Ed. with a memoir by Dorothy Livesay. Toronto: Ryerson, 1949.

————. "Nine Poems." *The Canadian Forum*, Sept. 1932, pp. 461-62.

————. "Elaine." *This Quarter*, 1, No. 1 (1925), 160-66.

————. "The Fate of Mrs. Lucier." *This Quarter*, 2, No. 2 (1925), 172-81.

————. "Mist-Green Oats." *The Midland*, No. 8 (Aug.-Sept. 1922), pp. 254-76.

————. "Peaches, Peaches." *The First Day of Spring: Stories and Other Prose*. Introd. Peter Stevens. Toronto: Univ. of Toronto Press, 1976.

————. "A Row of Horse Stalls." *This Quarter*, 1, No. 2 (1925), 30.

————. "Seven Poems." *The Midland*, No. 8 (Dec. 1922), pp. 329-32.

Koch, Vivienne. "Young Canadian's Poems." *New York Herald Tribune*, 7 Jan. 1945, Sec. 6, p. 12.

Layton, Irving. *The Improved Binoculars*. Introd. William Carlos Williams. Highlands: Jonathan Williams, 1956. 2nd ed. 1957.

————. "[A letter]." *The Canadian Forum*, Oct. 1956, pp. 160-62.

Leland, Charles G. *The Algonquin Legends*. Boston: Houghton, Mifflin & Co., 1884.

Lighthall, William Douw, ed. *Canadian Poets of the Great War*. Ottawa: Royal Society of Canada, [n.d.].

————, ed. *Songs of the Great Dominion: Voices from the Forests and Waters, the Settlements and Cities of Canada*. London: Walter Scott, 1889.

Livesay, Dorothy. *Day and Night*. Toronto: Ryerson, 1944.

————. Rev. of *Flight Into Darkness*, by Ralph Gustafson. *Contemporary Verse*, No. 14 (July 1945), pp. 15-16.

Macpherson, Jay. "The Fisherman: A Book of Riddles." *The Tamarack Review*, No. 1 (Autumn 1956), pp. 23-29.

————. "Plowman in Darkness." *The Canadian Forum*, March 1956, pp. 282-83.

Marriott, Anne. *The Wind Our Enemy*. Toronto: Ryerson, 1939.

Maugham, W. Somerset, ed. *Tellers of Tales: 100 Short Stories from the United States, England, France, Russia and Germany*. New York: Doubleday Doran &

Company, 1939.

McCullagh, Joan. *Alan Crawley and* Contemporary Verse. Vancouver: Univ. of British Columbia Press, 1976.

Moore, Marianne. "Modern Thoughts in Disguise." *Poetry* [Chicago], 42, No. 2 (May 1933), 114-15.

Morgan-Powell, S. "New Anthology Presents an Admirable Selection." *Montreal Star*, 25 July 1942, p. 18.

Morpurgo, J. E. *Allen Lane, King Penguin: A Biography*. London: Hutchinson, 1979.

Pacey, Desmond, ed. *A Book of Canadian Stories*. Toronto: Ryerson, 1947.

Pennell, Elizabeth Robins. *Charles Godfrey Leland: A Biography*. 2 vols. Boston and New York: Houghton, Mifflin and Company, 1906.

Pratt, E. J. *Collected Poems*. Toronto: Macmillan, 1944, and New York: Alfred A. Knopf, 1945.

———. *Newfoundland Verse*. Toronto: Ryerson, 1923.

Proud Procession. Toronto: Dent, 1947.

Purdy, A. W. "[A letter]." *The Canadian Forum*, Feb. 1957, p. 254.

Rand, Theodore H., ed. *A Treasury of Canadian Verse*. Toronto: William Briggs and London: Dent, 1900.

Reeve, Paul Eaton. "Malice: Foreshortened." *The New Act*, No. 1 (Jan. 1932), p. 16.

———. "Ode for Fly, Jr." *Fifth Floor Window*, 1, No. 4 (May 1932), n. pag.

Reviews of Ralph Gustafson's *A Little Anthology of Canadian Poets*, in *The New Republic*, 15 May 1944, p. 689; *New York Herald Tribune*, 9 Jan. 1944; and *The New Yorker*, 25 March 1944, p. 99.

Robins, John D., ed. *A Pocketful of Canada*. Toronto: Collins, 1946.

Rodman, Selden, ed. *A New Anthology of Modern Poetry*. Rev. ed. New York: The Modern Library, 1946.

Ross, W. W. E. "Air With Variations." *The Canadian Forum*, April 1957, p. 22.

———. "Anti-Archetypal." *Delta*, No. 3 (April 1958), p. 30.

———. "Distillates." In *New Directions in Poetry & Prose 1937*. Ed. James Laughlin IV. Norfolk: New Directions, 1937, pp. 125-29.

———. "Example." *Fifth Floor Window*, 1, No. 4 (May 1932), n. pag.

———. "Fall Wheat in Spring." *The New York Times*, 16 April 1964, p. 36.

———. "Falling Water." In *A Little Anthology of Canadian Poets*. Ed. Ralph Gustafson. Norfolk: New Directions, 1943, n. pag.

———. "Hart House Theatre." *Northern Review*, 7, No. 4 (Summer 1956), p. 20.

———. "Hypno II." *Fifth Floor Window*, 1, No. 4 (May 1932), n. pag.

———. "Irrealistic Verses." *Poetry* [Chicago], 44, No. 4 (July 1934), 179-84.

———. *Laconics*. Ottawa: Overbrook Press, 1930.

―――. "The Medici Tombs (Michelangelo)." *The New York Times*, 27 Feb. 1964, p. 30.

―――. "Morning." *Delta*, No. 8 (July 1959), p. 18.

―――. "Narration." *The Canadian Forum*, March 1952, p. 280.

―――. "News Report From Above." *Combustion*, No. 3 (July-Sept. 1957), p. 3.

―――. "On National Poetry." *The Canadian Forum*, July 1944, p. 88.

―――. "Seven Poems." *The Dial*, No. 85 (Aug. 1928), pp. 107-10.

―――. *Shapes & Sounds: Poems of W.W.E. Ross*. Ed. Raymond Souster and John Robert Colombo. Memoir by Barry Callaghan. Portrait by Dennis Burton. Don Mills: Longmans Canada Ltd., 1968.

―――. "[Six poems]." *Northern Review*, 4, No. 4 (April-May 1951), 6-11.

―――. "The Snake Trying." *Northern Review*, 7, No. 2 (Spring 1955), 27.

―――. *Sonnets*. Toronto: Heaton Publishing Co., 1932.

―――. "[Two poems]." *Delta*, No. 7 (April 1959), p. 5.

―――. "Two Poems." *The Dial*, No. 84 (April 1928), pp. 289-90.

Sandwell, B.K. Rev. of *Flight Into Darkness*, by Ralph Gustafson. *Saturday Night*, 3 Feb. 1945, p. 14.

Scott, Duncan Campbell. "A Dream." *Voices*, No. 113 (Spring 1943), pp. 6-8.

Scott, F.R. *The Eye of the Needle: Satires, Sorties, Sundries*. Montreal: Contact, 1957.

―――., and A.J.M. Smith, eds. *The Blasted Pine: An Anthology of Satire, Invective and Disrespective Verse Chiefly by Canadian Writers*. Preface by David L. Thomson. Toronto: Macmillan, 1957.

Scott, Winfield Townley. "Poetry and Event." *Poetry* [Chicago], 66, No. 6 (Sept. 1945), 329-34.

Smith, A.J.M., ed. *The Book of Canadian Poetry*. Chicago: Univ. of Chicago Press, 1943. Rev. ed. 1948; 3rd ed. 1957.

―――. "Canadian Anthologies, New and Old." *University of Toronto Quarterly*, 11, No. 4 (July 1942), 457-74.

―――. *The Classic Shade: Selected Poems*. Introd. M.L. Rosenthal. Toronto: McClelland and Stewart, 1978.

―――. "[A letter]." *The Canadian Forum*, Jan. 1957, p. 237.

―――. *News of the Phoenix and Other Poems*. Toronto: Ryerson, 1943, and New York: Coward-McCann, 1943 [i.e. 1944].

―――. "On Reading Certain Poems and Epistles of Irving Layton and Louis Dudek." *The Canadian Forum*, May 1957, pp. 41-42.

―――, ed. *The Oxford Book of Canadian Verse in English and French*. Toronto: Oxford Univ. Press, 1960.

―――. "The Recent Poetry of Irving Layton: A Major Voice." *Queen's Quarterly*, 62, No. 4 (Winter 1955-56), [587]-91.

Souster, Raymond. "Ersatz." *Voices*, No. 113 (Spring 1943), p. 39.

————. "The Hunter." *Voices*, No. 113 (Spring 1943), p. 39.

————. "Wild Night." *Voices*, No. 113 (Spring 1943), p. 38.

Stedman, Edmund Clarence, ed. *An American Anthology, 1787-1900: Selections Illustrating the Editor's Critical Review of American Poetry in the Nineteenth Century*. Cambridge: Riverside, 1900.

Stevens, Peter. "On W. W. E. Ross." *Canadian Literature*, No. 39 (Winter 1969), pp. 43-61.

Sutherland, John. "E. J. Pratt: A Major Contemporary Poet." *Northern Review*, 5, Nos. 3-4 (Feb.-March and April-May 1952), 36-64.

————. *Essays, Controversies and Poems*. Ed. Miriam Waddington. Toronto: McClelland and Stewart, 1972.

————. *The Poetry of E. J. Pratt: A New Interpretation*. Toronto: Ryerson, 1956.

"Talk of the Town." *The New Yorker*, 9 Oct. 1943, p. 15.

Tyler, Parker. "Prelude to Hollywood Dream Suite." *Fifth Floor Window*, 1, No. 4 (May 1932), n. pag.

————. "Shipshape Climber." *The New Act*, No. 1 (Jan. 1932), p. 23.

Whalley, George, ed. *Writing in Canada: Proceedings of the Canadian Writers' Conference, Queen's University, 28-31 July, 1955*. Introd. F. R. Scott. Toronto: Macmillan, 1956.

Williams, Oscar, ed. *A Little Treasury of Modern Poetry, English & American*. New York: Scribner's, 1946.